THE HOLOCAUST

THE HOLOCAUST

A GERMAN HISTORIAN EXAMINES THE GENOCIDE

WOLFGANG BENZ

TRANSLATED BY JANE SYDENHAM-KWIET

COLUMBIA UNIVERSITY PRESS

NEW YORK

Columbia University Press

Publishers Since 1893

New York   Chichester, West Sussex

Wolfgang Benz, *Der Holocaust* copyright 1995

© C. H. Beck'sche Verlagsbuchhandlung, München

Foreword copyright 1999 © Arthur Hertzberg

Copyright © 1999 Columbia University Press

Library of Congress Cataloging-in-Publication Data

Benz, Wolfgang. [Holocaust. English]   The Holocaust /

Wolfgang Benz; translated by Jane Sydenham-Kwiet.

p.   cm.   Includes bibliographical references and index.

ISBN 0–231–11214–9 (cloth.) — ISBN 0–231–11215–7 (pbk.)

1. Holocaust, Jewish (1939–1945).

2. Jews—Germany—History—1933–1945.

I. Title.   D804.3.B45413 1999

940.53'18—dc21   98–30726

Designed by Linda Secondari

c 10 9 8 7 6 5 4 3 2

p 10 9 8 7 6 5 4 3 2 1

CONTENTS

CONTENTS

FOREWORD
Arthur Hertzberg

Nearly two centuries ago Leopold von Ranke defined the task of the true historian as a commitment to describe the past "as it really was." That ideal has been challenged, and even derided, from many perspectives. Some have asked, What are the facts of history? Since not everything that once happened can be described and recorded, the historian must inevitably select some facts and discard many others. So the story that he tells is inevitably subjective. It reflects his values, his assessment of what matters and does not matter in human life. The attack on the possibility of objectivity is all the more pointed because so much of historical writing does not even bother to dissemble. Histories are often political pamphlets disguised with footnotes, especially when they are accounts of very controversial, and painful, events. In our own time the writing about the Holocaust is a prime example of this danger. Many historians have really become protagonists in the contemporary debates about the causes of the Holocaust and its extent. The debates are all the more heated and fierce when the issue becomes the assessing of responsibility.

There are "revisionist historians" who want us to

believe that the Holocaust never took place, and that the gas ovens in Auschwitz were disposal units for the bodies of those who had died in the camp from disease. This kind of "history" is almost universally decried as denial of the truth, but there is far greater division of opinion on the question of the sources of Nazism, or the responsibility of those who remained silent while six million Jews, and millions of other people, were being murdered by the Nazis and their helpers. Is Nazism unique to Germany, representing an exceptionally virulent tradition of anti-Semitism that reaches back at least to Martin Luther, or is it a mere accident that the Nazis appeared in Germany? Did those in occupied Europe who averted their eyes have any real choice, or could they have done much more to protect Jews? The questions are many and almost endless—but before one deals with any of these question, it is necessary to know what happened, and never mind all the criticism of Ranke's doctrine of absolute historical objectivity. There are some facts in history that cannot be talked out of existence by sophisticated theories about historians' subjectivity. The gas chambers were present at Auschwitz, and those who constructed them and used them committed a great and horrendous crime of mass murder, of death made into an industry based on modern technology. These events tower in their horror. They are indisputable and unavoidable facts of the history of our century.

A straightforward, short, but comprehensive account of

what happened in those years is a prime necessity. To be sure, the history of the Holocaust keeps being written and rewritten in great detail, and almost always by Jews, that is, by survivors or relatives of survivors. Wolfgang Benz's book is the first written by a German scholar of the younger generation to tell this story with exactness and absolute candor. It is astonishing that he has managed to tell so vast a story in a short book without ever giving the reader the feeling that he is compressing to get more facts into his account than its structure can bear. It is even more astonishing that Wolfgang Benz preaches no sermons and grinds no partisan axes. But there is profound moral passion, and great sorrow, between the lines of his book. In his last lines Benz refuses to participate in any of the speculations in which many of the fashionable historians have engaged. He leaves to others the prehistory of Nazism or speculations about the culpability of those who lived through the Nazi era. Benz seeks only to provide the basic and incontrovertible facts. Not a single line of this book can be contested or argued out of existence. All of these events took place, and they happened in the order in which he puts them.

Benz's account is the necessary "first course" for anyone who wants to know about the Holocaust and to think further about its meaning for humanity. It is of particular importance that the historian who has written this book is a German. This account is trustworthy because its author combines within himself the rare authority of someone who belongs to the past of his nation, both understanding and transcending its history in this century. The subject of the book, the Holocaust, is somber beyond words, but this account in Benz's words is cause for hope.

Arthur Hertzberg
February 1998

ACKNOWLEDGMENTS

This book would not have appeared in its present form without the invaluable work of its translator, Jane Sydenham-Kwiet, who has converted my German into a clearly articulated English, for which I am extremely grateful. Professor Konrad Kwiet has given me the benefit of his long scholarly experience in the study of the Holocaust and also provided me with the generous hospitality of MacQuarie University (Sydney). In addition to compiling the bibliography for this edition, Miriamne Fields contributed to the creation of the English version, ensuring that the book achieve and retain a high level of consistency. I would also like to thank the manuscript editor at Columbia University Press, Susan Pensak, for her excellent editorial assistance.

THE HOLOCAUST

1. TALKS FOLLOWED BY BREAKFAST:
The Wannsee Conference of January 20, 1942

Lined with villas, the quiet street Am Grossen Wannsee, counts itself among the finest addresses in Berlin. It was here that the Stiftung Nordhav (Nordhav Foundation) acquired the estate at numbers 56–58 at the end of the 1930s. The villa was intended to serve as a recreation center for members of the Security Service of the ss and their families. Founder and head of the foundation was Reinhard Heydrich. As chief of the Reich Security Main Office, the Security Police and Security Service of the Nazi state, he was one of the regime's most important men, more important than almost all the Reich ministers. Apart from Hitler, he received directions only from Göring, as the second highest officeholder in the regime, and from Reichsführer ss Heinrich Himmler, to whom he was directly accountable.

It was to the house on Am Grossen Wannsee on November 29, 1941, that Heydrich invited a number of high-ranking party functionaries to a roundtable discussion on the problems of a "total solution to the Jewish question in Europe." The meeting was originally to take place on December 9, but was canceled on short notice "due to events made known suddenly that laid claim to the time and expertise of some of the invited gentlemen."

On the January 20, 1942, the same group of participants was invited once again to a "talk followed by breakfast." On the agenda, disguised of course in bureaucratic jargon, was the singularly most monstrous crime committed in the history of mankind: the genocide of the Jews. For this reason the meeting at midday on January 20, 1942, is constantly misunderstood and seen as the occasion on which the "Final Solution"—genocide—was decided upon. That is incorrect. The Wannsee Conference was devoid of such a dramatic dimension and, indeed, the tragedy of the Jews' mass murder had already long been a reality. Moreover, any agreement on the extermination of millions of human beings would have gone far beyond the jurisdiction of those attending the talks. Nevertheless, the recorded minutes of that meeting, which was officially called a "state secretaries' discussion" and has been recorded in the annals of history as the Wannsee Conference, is a document central to the understanding of contemporary history. Invited to the meeting were thirteen men from the administration and executive of the Nazi state who, in their capacity as state secretaries and high-ranking officers, formed part of, roughly, the third rung in the hierarchy of leadership. Along with Heydrich, who dominated the meeting, and

2

Adolf Eichmann, his head of the Section on Jewish Affairs, who was responsible for recording the minutes of the meeting, and an unidentifiable shorthand typist, there were sixteen people gathered together.

The civil servants represented the Reich Ministries of the Interior and Justice, the Ministry for the Occupied Eastern Territories, the Reich Chancellery and the Party Chancellery of the NSDAP, the Foreign Office, the plenipotentiary of the Four-Year Plan and the governor general in Cracow. The SS officers were invited as members of the machinery of repression (Gestapo, Security Police, and SD) within the Reich as well as in the occupied territories in the East. Conspicuously absent were representatives of the Reich Ministry of Transport and the State Railways, as authorities important in the deportation of the Jews, as well as the Reich Finance Ministry, which oversaw the plundering of the Jews. Absent, too, was the army. Their presence at the meeting was in fact no longer necessary because cooperation between them was already running smoothly; indeed, in the East the army had been working alongside the SS-Einsatzgruppen in the massacres of the Jews since the beginning of the war. While the gentlemen were deep in discussion in the villa on Am Grossen Wannsee, the death commandos of the Einsatzgruppen had long been at work.

The matter under discussion in the Berlin villa remained within the abstract dimension of statistics. It can be assumed that those listening were not visualizing human beings when Reinhard Heydrich referred to the "over eleven million," scattered over all the countries of Europe, as a problem, namely, the Jewish question, to which a final solution must be found. Most certainly the civil servants and officers in the Wannsee villa were not thinking of individuals, of human beings, who were exposed to the most extreme humiliation and suffering and who in the moment of death must have despaired of God and humanity. The men at the discussion table were in high spirits; they followed Heydrich's explanations with lively interest, made suggestions, were generally in good humor. Adolf Eichmann, who acted as secretary and assisted Heydrich during the meeting, expressly confirmed that two decades later: "One was aware not only of a general atmosphere of enthusiastic agreement but beyond that of something completely unexpected, of what I would call a willingness that surpassed all expectations in respect to the final solution of the Jewish question." The convivial atmosphere lasted until the gentlemen had completed their talks, enjoyed breakfast together, and departed. A contented Heydrich stayed behind with Gestapo chief Müller and department head Eichmann. They sat together and drank cognac while Heydrich gave instructions as to how he wished the minutes of the meeting to be tabled.

The state secretaries' discussion had not lasted very long, perhaps an hour or two, certainly no longer (the exact length of the meeting is not documented anywhere), and there had been no objections raised nor contentious issues discussed. Had there been the expectation of a dramatic struggle, of at least a fight between the bureaucrats and the ss officers regarding the fate of the European Jews? Was Eichmann hinting at such in his description of the atmosphere at the end of the meeting during his trial in Jerusalem in spring 1960? "The general atmosphere was clearly reflected in Heydrich's relaxed and satisfied attitude. Without doubt he had reckoned with the greatest difficulties at this conference."

Eichmann, born in 1906, was one of the leading players within the bureaucracy of the murder of the Jews. Onward from 1932 he was a member of the NSDAP and the ss, from 1934 the expert on Jewish affairs within Himmler's Security Service (SD). As such he set up the Zentralstelle für jüdische Auswanderung (Main Office for Jewish Emigration) in Vienna in August 1938 and the Reichszentrale für jüdische Auswanderung (Reich Main Office for Jewish Emigration) in Berlin in October 1939. In these posts he gained experience in the expulsion and deportation of Jews; by 1941 he had become the leading expert in these matters.

SS-First Lieutenant Eichmann, head of Section IV B 4 (Jewish Affairs and Clearance Operations) within the Reich Security Main Office, who during interrogations in Israel never ceased to maintain what a small clog in the wheel of destruction he had been—a mere low-ranking bureaucrat—who at Wannsee sat quietly recording the minutes and listening to what his superiors had to say,

Eichmann, the lieutenant colonel and head of the Jewish Section within the Reich Central Police, maintained later too that the language used in the discussion had been clear and unambiguous. To be sure, he had had to refine the text of the minutes and to couch "certain excesses," a particular "jargon," in milder terms, or, rather, "in official language."

The relevant passages of the recorded minutes however still read as an uncoded text, at least to those that are familiar with the language of the ss state. In the minutes of the state secretaries' discussion that took place in the guest house on the Wannsee the fate of eleven million Jews is foretold in unambiguous terms. The central passage reads:

Within the course of the Final Solution and under the appropriate direction the Jews should be brought to work in the East in a fitting manner. Observing strict separation of the sexes, the Jews capable of work are to be led in large labor columns into these areas to build roads, whereby there is bound to be a large natural decline in numbers. The inevitable final remainder are to be treated in the appropriate manner, since they will undoubtedly represent the most resilient members of the group, the end product of the process of natural selection, who upon liberation will surely form the core of a new Jewish insurgence.

The total annihilation of the Jews throughout Europe, then, was pronounced as a matter that had long been decided upon, and at least half of those taking part in the discussions had a very clear idea of how the mass murders were being carried out or how they were yet to be executed. Of course they didn't need to use words like "killing," "gassing," or "shooting to death" (indeed, they did not even regard the planned annihilation of the Jews as murder). After all, they were educated and well-bred people or, at least, men of a certain standing, who had been brought together to conduct state business.

In any event, each of them was well aware of exactly what was meant by the terms *Aussiedlung* (resettlement), *Endlösung* (final solution), *Sonderbehandlung* (special treatment), and *Evakuierung* (evacuation).

At the beginning of the meeting Heydrich provided an overview of "the battle waged to date against this enemy." The goal set was "to rid all German territory of Jews by legal means." In the absence of an alternative, better means of achieving this aim the Jews had been compelled to emigrate, and this at their own expense. In the meantime the Reichsführer ss had outlawed the emigration of the Jews, "in view of the possibilities in the East." What indeed the telltale word *legal* meant when used by a high-ranking dignitary with special responsibilities when describing a state action nobody—not even State Secretary Freisler from the Reich Ministry for Justice—at the conference table thought to ask.

Left without any doubts as to what was being discussed and what was intended was the representative of the Foreign Office, Assistant State Secretary Martin Luther. In fact his office was at the time in the process of putting the governments of states under German control, states such as Croatia, Slovakia, Romania, Hungary, and Bulgaria under extreme pressure to persecute the Jews living within their borders and to hand them over to the Germans for deportation. In October 1941 a high-ranking official from the Foreign Office had even traveled to Belgrade to ascertain "whether in fact the problem of the eight thousand Jewish agitators whose deportation was demanded by the legation could not be solved then and there." A solution to the problem had already been found. At the end of October 1941 thousands of Serbian Jews and *Zigeuner* (gypsies) were shot dead not far from Belgrade. They were shot by the army, supposedly in a reprisal action. The first lieutenant responsible reported in great detail on the action ("The digging of the graves is most time consuming, the shooting itself proceeds very quickly: one hundred men every forty minutes—or—shooting the Jews is easier than shooting the gypsies"). The world was horrified. The Germans who chose to could learn that from a radio address given by Thomas Mann in London. Even before the Wannsee Conference Heydrich had made it known, and at the beginning of proceedings on January 20 he emphasized again, that the implementation of the "final solution of the Jewish question in Europe" was to be guided exclusively, centrally, and without regard to geographic boundaries from the office of the Reichsführer ss Himmler, in other words, by Heydrich himself, as Himmler's deputy.

With all the invitations Heydrich had included a photo-copy of his "certificate of appointment" in the form of an authorization dated July 31, 1941, and signed by Göring (an extrapolation and extension of the orders received in January 1939). The main purpose of the meeting was to make this fact clear to the high-ranking Reich authorities represented, in order to avoid counterproductive clashes of will in the common pursuit of achieving a Europe free of Jews. What was in question was the "Parallelisierung der Linienführung," as it was termed in the minutes of the meeting, the establishing of base lines and not organiza-tional and technical details. The discussion of these was left to follow-up meetings or they were relegated on the spot to the relevant authority—for example, transport problems related to the deportation to the State Railways.

Because the mass executions were so labor-intensive and costly, and took their toll on the nerves of the marks-men, those responsible were soon looking for alternative, more tolerable methods of murder. More tolerable, that is to say, for the murderers. To that end *Gaswagen* (mobile gas vans) had been put into operation in December 1941, shortly before the Wannsee Conference. In these vans up to sixty human beings could be killed at any one time on a short trip. One soldier who was an eyewitness reported:

They drove into the prison yard and the Jews, men, women, and children, had to climb into the vans directly from their cells. I am also familiar with the interior of the vans. They had metal fittings and a wooden grating on top. The exhaust fumes were fed into the interior of the van. Even today I can hear the knocking and screaming of the Jews: "Dear Germans, let us out."

Death in a gas van was slow and agonizing. But the murderers were highly satisfied with the method. The inspector of the gas vans reported as such to his superior office: "For instance, three vans in operation since December 1941 have processed 97,000 without any evidence of mechanical defects."

There was little discussion at the Wannsee villa. More than anything else the gentlemen took note of what Heydrich had to report. There is absolutely no question about the fact that his overview of the persecution of the Jews up until that point in time as well as of the continuing program as it was envisaged met with the enthusiastic approval of those assembled. The few interruptions were almost without exception of a pressing nature, like the request of State Secretary Bühler from Cracow to begin the Final Solution if possible in the General Government, on Polish territory. ss-Major General Hofmann from the ss Main Office for Race and Resettlement was outdone in his bid for wide-scale sterilization of *Mischlinge* (people of mixed race) by State Secretary Stuckart with his demand to resolve the issues of *Mischehen* (mixed marriages) and the offspring from these marriages once and for all through forced sterilization. In discussing how Mischlinge and the Jewish partners in Mischehen were to be treated in the future, the conference participants were breaking new ground. Until then this group of individuals, subdivided into various categories, had faced discrimination but had still been spared real threats to their physical existence. This was to change in the wake of Heydrich's exposition. Under discussion was an extension of the Nuremberg Laws, which provided the "legal" basis for the social exclusion of the Jews.

It was now intended that at some point those living in the relative security of Mischehen as well as their offspring should be included in the program of the Final Solution. To take this step required defining clearly who exactly was a "Jew," and who a "German." Heydrich's proposal in this matter of life and death, which would affect tens of thousands of human beings in the German Reich and hundreds of thousands throughout Europe, was that "Mischlinge of the first degree" be regarded as Jews as a matter of principle. On the other hand, "Mischlinge of the second degree" should in general be regarded as "of German blood."

It was intended that there be exceptions to this categorization. Mischlinge of the first degree who could demonstrate exceptional merit might be afforded equal standing with Germans. A prerequesite for this however would be "voluntary sterilization." By contrast, in the case of Mischlinge of the second degree, those who displayed a "racially exceptionally poor appearance" would be treated as Jews. In other words, they would be deported and murdered.

In fact, this debate on Mischlinge was to have no immediate consequences, but it demonstrated clearly the unswerving determination of the Nazi regime to murder methodically, cold-bloodedly, calculatedly, and with the full support of the bureaucracy every Jew it could lay its hands on. The Wannsee Conference stands as a clear piece of historical evidence to this intention.

The gas vans may have spared the nerves of the execution squads, but they proved inefficient. More effective methods were required for a genocidal campaign. Since September 1941 they had been on trial at the concentration camp in Auschwitz. Cyclon B, developed and used originally as a disinfectant, was quickly becoming a valuable tool in the trade of murder. The highly effective gas, containing prussic acid, which could easily be released from a silicic acid compound and posed no danger for the murderers, had first been used in the murder of the disabled within the "euthanasia program."

Since October 1941 the deportation trains of the German State Railways had been rolling through the countryside. Initially their destinations were the ghettos of Lodz and Riga, then Theresienstadt and other transit camps to the death camps in the East, in which the program that had been presented at the Wannsee Conference became a reality to a very large extent. Six million Jews (not fewer, most probably more) were murdered in the course of the Final Solution of the Jewish question, in what were virtually public massacres during the conquest of Polish, Soviet, and

Yugoslavian territory in the years 1939 to 1941 and then, from the end of 1941 to the end of 1944, with increasing perfection in the specially built extermination camps of Chelmno/Kulmhof, Auschwitz-Birkenau, Belzec, Sobibor, Treblinka, and Majdanek (Lublin).

What, in fact, had taken place at Am grossen Wannsee 56–58 on January 20, 1942, if indeed nothing was decided, if this meeting was not the beginning of the Holocaust? Gentlemen in uniform and gentlemen in civilian clothes had taken note of the intended murder of eleven million human beings, had discussed the possibilities of casting the net of victims even wider. As bureaucrats and functionaries they had performed their duty at the invitation of the highest ranking among them.

The gentlemen had dealt with the matter of genocide as an administrative matter. Caught up with other concerns as they were, they quickly forgot what they had been a party to. When in 1947 one of the, in total, thirty copies of the minutes of the meeting had surfaced, those participants at the conference who could be located were interrogated. The interrogations fell under the jurisdiction of a former Prussian civil servant who, as a Jew, had been able to emigrate in time. Now Robert Kempner was an American and worked for the prosecution within the Nuremberg military tribunal. State Secretary a. D. Neumann, who had represented the Office of the Plenipotentiary of the Four-Year Plan at the Wannsee Conference, denied his participation at the meeting. Like his colleague, Klopfer, from the Party Chancellery, who claimed to have known nothing about the murderous persecution of the Jews (only "resettlement" had been discussed), Neumann retracted to a position of protesting that in his work he had had nothing to do with Jewish affairs. Kempner drew his attention to the fact that on January 20 he was the only one to have offered something in the Jews' favor: those forced laborers who were working within the armaments industry should in his opinion only be deported when replacements had been found for them.

2. GERMAN JEWS AND NATIONAL SOCIALISM:
Self-Image and Threat

At the time of the National Socialist seizure of power there were somewhat more than half a million people living in the German Reich who declared themselves Jews and viewed themselves as a religious minority (.76 percent of the total population). A noteworthy characteristic of this minority was that its members were represented disproportionately in certain professions, above all in the areas of commerce (including real estate and banking), in the medical and legal professions, and in the arts and cultural studies. There were long-standing social and political reasons for this phenomenon, reasons for which the Jews themselves shared the least blame. The traditional hostility against the Jews, with its social discrimination that far transcended the formal conferring of equal rights before the law during the period of emancipation, was little concerned with what was cause and what effect. Equally of no interest to antisemites was how the Jews in fact lived in Germany as a religious and cultural minority; what mattered to them was solely the distorted image of a parasitic band of usurers and hagglers, strange beings who were ill-disposed to everything German and who could be used as a political instrument.

Worse still than this depiction of Jewishness in the National Socialist propaganda based on conscious caricature or intentional misunderstanding were of course the conspiracy theories, which were built on social jealousy and used the well-situated Jews, who in no way formed a majority, as their starting point in claims of machinations of a "world Jewry" against the Germans. These claims found particular resonance among the lower middle classes and the impoverished members of the middle class because they provided a simple explanation for the hitherto impenetrable causes of the economically disastrous inflation of 1923. The Jew had dared to "declare war on the Germans. With the help of the Jewish-controlled press he was engaged throughout the world in a campaign of lies against a Germany that had rediscovered its nationalism," it was declared, at the call for a mass rally at the Königsplatz in Munich on the eve of the boycott of Jewish shops and factories, which had been fixed for April 1, 1933.

Less crude perhaps but no less false was the accusation directed at the Jews that they were living in dual loyalty, first as Jews and then as Germans. Equally incorrect was the assertion that the Jewish minority formed a socially, culturally, politically, and intellectually unified group that shared the same convictions, behavioral patterns, and reactions in the face of the threats that found their expression in Nazi propaganda.

With the wave of "national awakening" at the beginning of 1933 antisemitism of the very worst variety had become official state doctrine. Antisemitism was used to consolidate the power of the new ruling elite and was systematically employed to morally discredit the Jewish minority in Germany, to defame its members socially, and to discriminate against them in legal terms. In the first weeks following Hitler's seizure of power it was simply unimaginable to the well-educated German Jew that the civil rights and economic existence of the German Jews could be destroyed by National Socialism, far less that even worse could befall them.

The Jewish boycott, announced by the NSDAP at the end of March and put into practice on April 1, 1933, brought with it for the Jews, after weeks of dreadful foreboding, the first real shock and the first sign that the National Socialists would not let it rest with their usual declarations of antisemitism. That was what the Jews had been hoping until the NSDAP used the "horror propaganda" of a foreign Jewish press (from which the Jewish organizations in Germany distanced themselves in despair) as an excuse to make very clear to the Jews as well as to the largely not particularly antisemitic non-Jewish population what the general direction of the official policy toward the Jews would be in the future.

The objections and protestations, which were put to paper by Jewish officials at the end of March, comprised a mixture of earnest rejections "of the monstrous accusations that have been made against us German Jews," of a resolute distancing from the foreign press, which through its reporting on Jewish policy provided Hitler's government the grounds for such accusations, as well as of appeal for reason and propriety. Not one of these documents, which were sent to government agencies at all levels including to the Reich Chancellery, failed to make reference to the twelve thousand Jewish fallen in World War I. In August 1933 the Reichsbund jüdscher Frontsoldaten (Reich League of Jewish War Veterans), which was formed after World War I and demonstrated a deliberately nationalistic stance, declared emphatically the right of German Jews to live in the German Reich as citizens with equal rights in a special edition of its association's newsletter, *Der Schild*. As proof of the association's basic attitude, it staged a patriotic address endorsing Germany's withdrawal from the League of Nations.

The recognition that the foundation of Jewish life in Germany was shattered was not particularly widespread in spring 1933. Of course the shock of the Jewish boycott strengthened the authority of the Zionists, who could point to the fact that they obviously were, and indeed had been for a long time, on the right track in propagating a boosting of Jewish self-awareness and the founding of a Jewish nation on Palestinian soil. The more radical the Nazi state became, and the more threatening the situation for the Jews in Germany, the greater the persuasive power of the Zionists became. The editorials in the *Jüdischer Rundschau,* which called for a revitalization of Judaism, provided even many non-Zionists in the period following with moral support. Under the title "Ja-Sagen zum Judentum" (Say Yes to Judaism), it was noted that the community spirit among Jews had become stronger. Jewish individuals, who, only a short time ago, had either not heeded each other or been indifferent to each other had become closer. "Fellow Jews are felt to be companions in misfortune, brothers. Jewish people can talk to each other again." It must not be assumed from this that *die Juden,* the Jews in Germany, formed a cohesive group in terms of their philosophy of life and political attitudes. On the contrary, the supporters of the Zionistische Vereinigung für Deutschland (Zionist Federation of Germany)—their numbers were not very significant—were accused by the very large group representing the assimilationists, the Central-Verein (CV) deutscher Staatsbürger jüdischen Glaubens (Central Association of German Citizens of the Jewish Faith), of advocating an isolationist policy and a "return to the ghetto."

Further differences were evident in the religious sphere, between the (few) Orthodox, the Conservative, and the Liberal, or Reform, Jews; the majority of Jews demonstrated relative indifference toward their religion. Like many Christians they kept some outward customs and observed the High Holy Days; beyond that, however, they did not permit religion to impinge on their day-to-day existence.

It was the threat from outside then that forged the alliance between groups of differing political orientation. The aim from spring 1933 was to establish an umbrella group that would represent the political interests of all the Jewish organizations, raise awareness of Jewish culture, and also take on the role of a welfare organization by offering financial assistance to all those who required it by virtue of being Jews. The founding of the Zentralausschuss für Hilfe und Aufbau (Central Agency for Relief and Reconstruction) in April 1933 marked a beginning at the economic and social welfare levels. All the important Jewish organizations were represented: the cv, the Zionist Union of Germany, the Prussian Sate Association of Jewish Communities, the Jewish Community of Berlin, the Jewish Women's Association, and the Orthodox state organization, Agudas Jisroel. The new Central Committee was presided over by the prominent rabbi Leo Baeck; its direction was determined, however, by younger men like the general secretary, Max Kreutzberger, who emigrated to Palestine in 1935, Salomon Adler-Rudel, who was expelled from Germany in 1936, and Friedrich Brodnitz, who emigrated to the United States in 1937. His successor, Paul Eppstein, was murdered in Theresienstadt in 1944. In the six years until 1938/1939—all the time it was left with— the Central Committee constituted an impressive self-help organization whose activities spanned all spheres of life. It was financed by the Jewish communities throughout the German Reich but also received substantial financial support from foreign relief agencies like the American Joint Distribution Committee and the Central British Fund. It also profited from the collections of the Jüdische Winterhilfe (Jewish Winter Relief Agency).

In the face of the continuing economic and social discrimination of the Jews in Germany the Central Committee was never short of work. After the passing of the Nuremberg Laws the area of education and training became a high priority. Through its own Jewish School System not only could Jewish self-awareness and community spirit be fostered but at the same time emigration could be promoted through training in practical professions and instruction in Hebrew. Needless to say, preparation for emigration and assistance for those prepared to emigrate played a major role. So too however the measures taken to retrain those who had been forced out of their professions—those who had been dismissed from the public service or from jobs within the media, etc., or members of the free professions who had suddenly found themselves without work. They were given the opportunity to acquire practical knowledge and skills that would help secure their future economic existence. Because the German Jews were being increasingly excluded from the public social welfare system the Central Committee for Relief and Reconstruction found itself having to take over the whole range of welfare work and financial aid, and that during a time of rapidly increasing impoverishment of the German Jews. Money lending, job search, health care, care of the aged, institutionalized care and care of war victims were given priority within the organizational planning. The achievements of the Central Committee were admirable and clearly demonstrated self-assertiveness and solidarity in the face of an environment that was becoming more threatening from day to day.

Equally remarkable were the initiatives in cultural and intellectual life, which, from the middle of July 1933 were overseen by the Kulturbund Deutscher Juden (Cultural League of German Jews). The Kulturbund, within which Kurt Singer (medical practitioner and musician and, until spring 1933, director of the Städtische Oper in Berlin), the young director Kurt Baumann, the music critic Julius Bab, and many others worked with devotion, also had a social function in the form of providing assistance to artists. It offered dismissed Jewish musicians, actors, and other artists work and an audience. The Cultural Association of German Jews (which from 1935 on, when the Jews were no longer permitted to call themselves German, was called the Reichsverband der Jüdischen Kulturbände Deutschland—

Reich Association of the Jewish Cultural Organizations of Germany—and from 1938 to 1941 was still active under the name Jüdischer Kulturbund in Deutschland—Jewish Cultural Association in Germany) saw itself primarily as a manifestation of a self-assured and—at least in intellectual terms—self-assertive German Jewry. Despite all the conflicts in regard to its programming, which dogged the Kulturbund throughout its short history, it remained the most important bastion of German-Jewish assimilation.

The Kulturbund, as an organization that recruited members and membership, meant for many German Jews the only opportunity to take part in any form of communal cultural life, once they were denied access to and participation in German cultural life. Of course the opportunity was greater in Berlin and other major cities in the German Reich. Moreover the Kulturbund was a cultural ghetto in which the Jews sought relaxation and comfort.

The greatest problem that German Jewry faced in its self-portrayal was the mantle of commonality placed around its politically, sociologically, and religiously diverse organizations, groups, and movements, a mantle that had been woven at the last possible moment and with a sense of urgency under the pressure of prevailing circumstances. There had been various hurdles to the amalgamation of the different associations and organizations, an amalgamation that would have allowed German Jewry to speak with one voice even before Hitler's seizure of power. There were of course the religious differences between the

Orthodox, Liberal, and Conservative communities. There was also, however, the awareness of the significance of federalism on the part of the South German state associations, which was at odds with the organizational ideas of the Prussian State Association of Jewish Communities. There were the differing and always stridently expressed interests of the large associations, the cv and the Zionist Federation of Germany, but also those representing the particular orientation of the Reich League of Jewish War Veterans, not to mention the smaller groups and sects.

By September 1933 the amalgamation had been achieved and President Baeck published the program of the Reichsvertretung der Deutschen Juden (Reich Agency of German Jews). Basically he saw this organization as having three tasks: ensuring that school and vocational training be conducted in the spirit of Judaism, securing the economic existence of those it represented, and promoting emigration from Germany.

The Reich Agency of German Jews—from 1935 onward operating under the changed name of Reichsvertretung der Juden in Deutschland (Reich Association of Jews in Germany)—represented the interests of the German Jews until 1943. Following the November pogrom of 1938, however, it no longer functioned as a freely elected body with this name but as the Reichsvereinigung der Juden in Deutschland (Reich Association of Jews in Germany), a body ordained and set up by the National Socialist apparatus of power. But even in the organization's executive (of which Leo Baeck was the chairman) there were four men appointed by the Security Police who had been there from the moment of amalgamation in 1933. The Reichsvereinigung carried on its work until June 10, 1943, in the face of numbers decimated by arrests and emigration and continuing harassment and discrimination at the hands of the Gestapo. On this day it was closed by the Gestapo, and the last staff members, among them Leo Baeck, were deported to Theresienstadt. The very worst form of discrimination had come at the end: the positions of those who represented German Jewry from 1935 onward were increasingly abused by compelling the men in them to provide administrative assistance in the National Socialist persecution of the Jews. The attitude of the Jews can not be characterized alone by acceptance of the National Socialist measures; the opportunities for assertiveness and resistance, however, were few and, in the course of time, became even fewer, not least because of the dwindling readiness for solidarity among non-Jews.

3. EXCLUSION AND DISCRIMINATION OF THE JEWS IN GERMANY, 1933–1939

It was only two months after the seizure of power in 1933 that Hitler's government passed the Gesetz zur Wiederherstellung des Berufsbeamtentums (Law for the Restitution of the German Civil Service) in April 1933. The law achieved exactly the opposite of what its name suggested: it served as an instrument to remove all political opponents from the public service, including all public servants of Jewish origin. By analogy the "Aryan clause" was also applied in the period following in all professional associations as well as in many other organizations, thus ensuring the exclusion of the Jews.

In April 1933 a Gesetz gegen die Überfüllung der deutschen Schulen und Hochschulen (Law to Prevent the Overcrowding of German Schools and Tertiary Institutions) also served to place a strict quota on the number of Jews attending educational institutions. This was a step on the way to total exclusion. In October 1933, with the help of a Schriftleitergesetz (Editorial Law), the Jews were removed from jobs within the media. In May 1935 all Jews were excluded from the army, and in September 1935 the Nuremberg Laws were passed. The first of these laws, the Reichsbürgergesetz (Reich Citizen Law) turned the Jews into second-class citizens and the other, the Gesetz zum Schutz des deutschen Blutes und der deutschen Ehre (Law to Protect German Blood and German Honor) proscribed among other things marriage between Jews and non-Jews. (Sexual relations outside of marriage were outlawed from this time on as "racial defilement" and punished severely). In themselves the Nuremberg Laws were harsh enough, but they also functioned as an instrument for further discrimination. Above all the Reich Citizen Law, in conjunction with the endless decrees and regulations governing its implementation and enforcement, served again and again to limit the rights of the Jewish minority.

From March 1936 there was no longer any financial assistance for Jewish families with several children; in October 1936 Jewish teachers were forbidden to give private tutoring to non-Jews. This, in effect, often robbed the teachers concerned of the last source of income left to them after they had been forbidden to work in the public service. From 1937 Jews could no longer attain a doctorate at universities; in September 1937 Jewish doctors had their accreditation with all health insurers withdrawn; in July 1938 they lost their license to practice medicine. Within a short time the same fate befell lawyers and other professional groups.

At the end of April 1938 all Jews were compelled to publicly declare their assets; in May Jews were forbidden to accept a public tender; in August a decree was passed that made the addition of the first name Sara or Israel mandatory; at the beginning of October the Jews were further stigmatized by having a red *J* stamped in their passports; from the middle of November Jewish children were no longer permitted to attend German schools. These were by no means the only measures taken against the Jewish population, which was also exposed to harassment and discrimination at a local level: the signs at entrances stating clearly that Jews were undesirable, the park benches with the inscription "Only for Aryans," the banning from local swimming facilities, and many other things.

By Autumn 1938, after five and a half years of National Socialist rule, the living conditions of the German Jews had worsened dramatically as the result of discriminatory measures planned and executed by the state. Many were unable to believe that things could get even worse, others, however, were convinced that the openly declared threat of a "solution to the Jewish question" would be carried out. Yet, after everything that had already happened, nobody was prepared to believe that the situation would culminate in a spontaneous outburst of public fury, as by all accounts was the case on the November 9, 1938.

As was often the case in the history of the Nazi state, it was a peripheral event, an insignificant catalyst, that set the fateful development in motion. In March 1938, following the Anschluss (annexation) of Austria, the Polish government called into question the validity of the passports of all expatriate Poles if they had lived abroad continuously for more than five years and had lost all ties with the Polish state. In spring 1938 there were fears in Warsaw that the approximately twenty thousand Jews of Polish nationality, who had been living in Austria for a long time but who would now probably not wish to come under National Socialist rule, would return to Poland.

The Polish law was passed on March 31, 1938, but was not yet put into force. It was only on October 15, directly following the Munich Agreement, that a Polish decree was issued enforcing the scrutiny of all passports belonging to expatriate Poles. From October 31 all consulate passports—in other words, all documents issued abroad—would only entitle the bearer to enter Poland after the addition of a special stamp at a Polish consulate. This directly affected the fifty thousand Polish Jews who were living in the German Reich, many of whom had been living there for decades. It was the clear intention of the government in Poland that the majority of them should become stateless at the end of October, on October 30, to be precise. After that the German Reich government would no longer have the option of deporting their troublesome Eastern Jews across the eastern border, as Poland no longer recognized them as citizens.

After negotiations between Berlin and Warsaw failed—the Poles had twice refused to allow holders of Polish passports without the special stamp across the border after October 30—the Foreign Office, on October 26, handed the matter over to the Gestapo with the result that all Polish Jews were to be deported within the next four days. The Gestapo set to work without delay and with extreme brutality. Approximately seventeen thousand Jews were deported to the Polish border and then forced across. After Poland closed the border, they were forced to wander back and forth in a no-man's-land between Germany and Poland. The Grünspan family was among those Jews who found themselves with an invalid passport. One son, seventeen-year-old Herschel, was living in Paris at the time and so escaped deportation. On November 3 he received a postcard from his sister with a description of what had befallen them.

A few days later the stateless youth, who was roaming about Paris illegally, triggered off events the dimensions of which he could not have begun to guess at. His shooting of an official of the German Embassy in Paris became the catalyst for the pogrom that indeed marked the turning point. Through no other event did the Nazi regime demonstrate so cynically that it no longer attached any importance to even the appearance of upholding law and order. Antisemitism and animosity against the Jews, propagated from the beginning as an integral part of National Socialist ideology, now found their expression in the most primitive forms of violence and persecution. The Reichskristallnacht represented the vertex on the path to the Final Solution, to the systematic murder of millions of Jews from all over Europe.

The November pogrom of 1938 was far from a spontaneous outburst; it was staged by state bodies at the highest level. The immediate trigger for the pogrom had been provided by Herschel Grünspan, who on November 7 had shot and seriously wounded the third secretary in the German Embassy in Paris, Ernst vom Rath. With this act Herschel Grünspan had wanted to protest against the brutal deportation of the Jews of Polish nationality from German soil at the end of October 1938. The suffering of his family had been his motive, nothing more. Speculation as to whether Grünspan and vom Rath knew each other and whether there were in fact very private motives for Grünspan's assassination attempt are neither relevant nor can they be proven. Decisive for the events that followed were not the assassin and his victim but rather (as in the case of the Reichstagsbrand—the setting on fire of the German parliament—of 1933) the opportunities that such an act provided the National Socialists.

The National Socialists welcomed the act in no uncertain terms. It was skillfully turned into an act representing the conspiracy of "world Jewry" against the German Reich and served to usher in the final phase of the exclusion of German Jews from all social and economic spheres of life. First Goebbels used the assassination attempt as the basis for an antisemitic press campaign. The nationwide staged pogrom began after Goebbels's speech in front of the "old guard" of the NSDAP on the evening of November 9 in the Old Town Hall in Munich. As on this day every year, the leaders of the NSDAP had gathered in Munich to commemorate Hitler's putsch of 1923. At 9 P.M. came the news of vom Rath's death. At about 10 P.M., after Hitler had left the gathering, stimulation for the leaders of the NSDAP and SA was provided by the Reich propaganda chief, who spoke of retaliation and revenge and gave the impression that they were called upon to action. Via regional (Gau) propaganda offices and from them to the district and local party headquarters or the SA staff throughout the Reich, the general mood was passed on by telephone, already now in the form of an order. A short time later the first synagogues were burning; everywhere Jewish people were being humiliated, derided, mistreated, plundered.

Things did not stop, however, with this public and seemingly spontaneous vandalism. In the days following November 9, 1938, approximately thirty thousand Jewish men, predominantly those situated well financially, were arrested throughout the German Reich and sent to the three concentration camps Dachau, Buchenwald, and Sachsenhausen. What this meant for the people concerned is barely describable despite the numerous eyewitness reports. The fact that the action was limited to a few weeks, that it was intended to intimidate and to exert pressure to emigrate and not (yet) to annihilate the Jews, counted for little in the face of the catastrophe that time spent in a concentration camp represented for respectable middle-class existences, for the destruction of familiar life patterns, and in the consciousness of the victims.

On November 12, directly following the pogrom of November 9, which came to be known under the harmless sounding name of Reichskristallnacht (literally, "Reich Crystal Night," or, as it was later termed in English, Night of Broken Glass), stock was taken of the material damage sustained during the nationwide action. At a conference held in Berlin under the chairmanship of Hermann Göring, Hitler's right-hand man, it was confirmed that 7,500 Jewish shops were reported destroyed, almost all synagogues had been burnt down or destroyed (according to official records, 191 Jewish houses of worship were destroyed by fire, a further 76 through acts of human violence; more recent research reveals that far more than 1,000 synagogues and houses of worship fell victim to the pogrom), and shop windows to the value of many millions of marks were smashed in the night from November 9 to 10. The number of deaths as the result of murder, mistreatment, terror, and despair lay in the hundreds, excluding suicide victims.

At the time of the conference the preparations for the final phase of the exclusion of the Jews from economic life were already completed: in April 1938 a decree was passed making it compulsory for Jews to register all property valued in excess of 5,000 Reichsmark; beginning in June Jewish businesses were to be identifiable as such as a means of initiating their "Aryanization." On October 14, at a conference on the production aims of the scheduled wide-scale economic and armaments program, Göring declared that "the Jewish question must now be addressed with all means at our disposal, because they must be removed from economic life." In the meeting on November 12 the future direction of National Socialist policy regarding the Jews was laid down. In the following days and weeks this policy received the full backing of Goebbels's propaganda machine, being declared in keeping with the will of the people, namely, first the expropriation, then the ghettoization, and finally the deportation and annihilation of those German Jews who were not fortunate enough to escape

German territory in time. By November 10 the decision had already been made in favor of the expropriation of the Jews, the complete Aryanization of the German economy decided upon by Hitler. Contentious remained above all the issue of who should pocket the profits, the state or the NSDAP. Göring, as the plenipotentiary for the Four-Year Plan, held sway over the Reich minister for propaganda, who had wanted to fill the party's coffers with the money taken from the Jews. The ministers and officials were in agreement that the Jews should not only accept liability for the damage caused during the pogrom—whereby they indeed suffered severe losses, since the insurance payments to which they were duly entitled were confiscated by the regime—but that a "fine" should also be imposed on the German Jews. There was little discussion required on the amount of the fine: 1 billion Reichsmark. At the end the Jews were in fact forced to pay 1.12 billion.

By November 12 the complete Aryanization of at first all Jewish retail shops, then of all factories and shares was a foregone conclusion, a matter that had been decided upon by Hitler himself before the gentlemen discussed measures that would ensure once and for all the exclusion and isolation of the Jews from German society. Suggestions ranged from a prohibition against entering German forests to the removal of all synagogues in favor of parking lots, from regulations regarding the use of trains to the banning of Jews from public parks and the wearing of a distinguishing costume as in the Middle Ages (Göring considered uniforms most appropriate) or, at the very least, a special badge.

Most of these suggestions were put into practice in the weeks and months that followed when, directly following the pogrom, the total deprivation of rights of the Jews was initiated through a series of instructions and decrees, orders and prohibitions. Physical destruction constituted then the final stage of the course that had been consciously and publicly adopted in November 1938.

4. JEWISH EMIGRATION, 1933–1941

A question that is often asked is why the Jews did not escape the oppression and harassment through timely emigration. Apart from the fact that the majority of German Jews, no less than other Germans, felt themselves bound to the German homeland and culture and for that reason felt no inclination to emigrate, there were also considerable difficulties associated with emigration. The Nazi state both pushed for and restricted the emigration of the German Jews at the same time. On the one hand, exclusion from economic life gave impulse to the will to emigrate, on the other hand, the confiscation of assets and the crippling fees limited the possibilities for emigration. No country accepting immigrants is interested in impoverished newcomers, and a particularly insidious aspect of the regime was that it hoped to export antisemitism whenever the Jews driven out of Germany threatened to become a social problem in their adoptive countries.

In July 1938 an international conference devoted to the problems of Jewish migration from Germany was held on the French bank of Lake Geneva. President Roosevelt had issued the invitations; guests included representatives from thirty-two countries and many Jewish organizations. Apart from the establishment of an Intergovernmental Committee for Refugees based in London, and the vague assurance from some countries that their existing emigrant quotas could be filled in the future, nothing in fact took place here to improve the chances for emigration of Jews out of Hitler's sphere of power.

The responsible authority in Berlin was in the first instance the Reich Office for Emigration Within the Reich Ministry for the Interior. In January 1939 the Reichszentrale für jüdische Auswanderung (Reich Central Office for Jewish Emigration) was founded along the same lines as the office set up by Adolf Eichmann in Austria. It fell under the control of the chief of the Security Police, Reinhard Heydrich, was officially a department of the Reich Ministry for the Interior, and was de facto identical with section 2 of the Gestapo.

The emigration policy of the Nazi regime was inconsistent and inscrutable: an increased pressure to emigrate at the beginning of 1939 was followed by enormous obstructions and finally by a total emigration ban in Autumn 1941. Encouraged was emigration to Palestine, for which there were complicated arrangements for the transfer of capital (the Haavara Agreement) and illegal immigrant aid. By contrast, emigration to neighboring European countries was obstructed. It seemed reasonable that the Jewish refugees fleeing Hitler in the first wave of emigration first made their way to neighboring districts. The Saarland, which was under the mandate of the League of Nations until 1935, was the first place of refuge for many, as were Austria and Czechoslovakia, which on balance were kindlier disposed toward the emigrants than Switzerland. The most important country of exile in 1933/1934 was France. Needless to say, the economic situation there was bleak and not a few Jews, grown weary of the tiring and seemingly hopeless quest for a new existence, returned to Germany. A French law passed in November 1934 decisively limited the earning possibilities for foreigners; the same occurred in Belgium, to which a move was made much more difficult in February 1935. The small country of Luxembourg offered refuge until the German invasion in May 1940; between twenty-five to thirty thousand German Jews found a short-term sanctuary in the Netherlands. Fascist Italy also offered possibilities for escape, even beyond September 20, when under pressure from the Germans Mussolini introduced legislation regarding the Jews that gradually came to resemble the Nuremberg Laws. In Italy—and similarly in Spain where the fascist Franco was in power—there was a lack of real antisemitic convictions among the people, and passing the racial laws did not necessarily mean their strict observance.

Because Great Britain, unlike most of Europe's countries of exile, did not in time come under German rule, it retained the greatest percentage of German Jewish immigrants both for a limited period and indefinitely. By April 1938 about eleven thousand Jews had sought refuge in the British Isles, a further forty thousand were permitted to come after the Night of Broken Glass. Generous was the help offered to Jewish children in the wake of the November pogrom. Thousands could be saved through the children's transports.

The most important and sought-after countries of exile were Palestine and the United States. For different reasons, however, it was difficult to reach them. Palestine was a British mandate and the Zionists eager to emigrate there, generally young Jews who together prepared themselves for their existence as new settlers, were allowed in only in small numbers according to a complicated quota system. The number of Jews who emigrated to Palestine legally, that is, under the official supervision of the Jewish Agency, was no more than twenty-nine thousand between 1933 and 1936 and about eighteen thousand in the years 1937 to 1941. Illegal immigration (Aliyah Bet) was a highly risky affair and a successful escape route for only a few thousand people in total.

Immigration quotas also constituted for many the

insurmountable hurdle barring their entry to the United States of America. Yet up until 1939 the yearly quotas were not even filled. Reasons for this were both the strict control of currency exchange in Germany and the restrictive policy of the American immigration authorities. After the November pogrom the restrictions were eased, but for many it was too late. If at first it was the fear of being troubled by poor Jews from Central Europe that can explain the restrictions, after the outbreak of war there was the additional concern that Nazi spies could infiltrate the ranks of the would-be immigrants. There were in any case considerable barriers to overcome before permission to immigrate into the United States was granted. Despite this fact the United States remained the most important country of exile: more than 130,000 German and Austrian Jews found refuge there.

What awaited the Jews who had fled Germany was an arduous daily existence beset with considerable problems of adjustment, communication barriers, professional decline, financial distress, and feelings of having been uprooted—a state that remained with many until the end of their lives. In 1939 more Jews than in any other year succeeded in escaping Nazi Germany: the figure lies somewhere between seventy-five and eighty thousand. In 1940 fifteen thousand were able to flee, in 1941 a further eight thousand. On October 23, 1941, emigration was prohibited. At this point the genocidal campaign was already being waged.

5. ARYANIZATION AND THE JEWISH STAR:
German Jews Are Totally Stripped of Their Civil Rights,
1939–1941

In Autumn 1938, at the time of the November pogrom, forty thousand of the originally one hundred thousand Jewish businesses were still in the hands of their rightful owners. The Aryanization measures had been most keenly felt within the retail trade: of approximately fifty thousand shops only nine thousand remained. The number of unemployed Jews had continued to rise, professional bans and forced sales had led to widespread impoverishment. The Verordnung zur Ausschaltung der Juden aus dem deutschen Wirtschaftsleben (decree expelling Jews from the German financial sector) passed on November 12, 1938, destroyed those existences that were still intact. From January 1, 1939, Jews were forbidden to run retail businesses, to sell goods and offer commercial services at markets and public festivities, and to operate trade services.

As a general rule the businesses passed into the hands of non-Jewish owners for a percentage of what they were worth (so-called Aryanization) or they were dissolved. Either way this spelled financial ruin for the Jewish owner because he had no control over the proceeds of the sale, which were paid into blocked accounts and later confiscated to the coffers of the German Reich. Jews were forced to sell all precious objects, jewelry, and antiques at well below their real value. Jews were also no longer permitted to own stocks and shares: they were deposited into a compulsory depot. In addition, all Jewish real estate was *zwangsarisiert*—in other words, passed into the hands of non-Jewish owners. Jewish employees were sacked; with few exceptions, self-employed Jews were subject to professional bans. Of 3,152 doctors only 709 were permitted to look after exclusively Jewish patients as "carers of the sick," and this permission could be revoked at any time.

The increasing impoverishment of the German Jews was used by the authorities to introduce forced labor. The relevant decree from the president of the Reich Office for Employment and Unemployment Benefits was passed on December 20, 1938; from that time on, all Jews fit to work were exploited in the most discriminatory fashion—*abgesondert von der Gefolgschaft* (removed from the workforce) for *staatspolitisch wichtigen Vorhaben* (projects of political significance), by which was meant predominantly factories serving the armaments industry.

With the outlawing of Jewish newspapers and organizations after the November pogrom the public life of the Jews was brought to a standstill. Plundered and left destitute, they found themselves with nothing outside their private existences, led under increasingly wretched conditions and subject to new and ongoing harassment. On April 30 the Gesetz über Mietverhältnisse mit Juden (Law Concerning Rental Relations with Jews) heralded the preparations for the accommodating of Jewish families together in "Jewish houses." The intention was—and it was quickly put into practice—to crowd as many Jews as possible together under one roof, thus making surveillance (and later deportation) an easier matter. The measure was justified on the grounds that "Aryans" could not be expected to live in the same building as Jews.

The outbreak of war on September 1, 1939, brought with it a curfew: Jews were no longer permitted to leave their homes after 9 P.M. in summer and after 8 P.M. im winter. From September 20 they were forbidden to own radio receivers, a measure made necessary by war, it was claimed. This was the same justification offered when on July 19, 1940, Jews were prohibited from owning telephones—they were regarded after all as "enemies of the Reich." From as early as the beginning of December 1938 they had been forbidden to drive a car or to own a vehicle, from September 1939 they were permitted to buy groceries only in specifically designated stores, and from July 1940 the Jews of Berlin were allowed to do their grocery shopping between 4 P.M. and 5 P.M. only (their allotted rations being in addition considerably fewer than those of the "Aryans"). Resourceful bureaucrats were always coming up with new and pernicious measures, such as the prohibition against keeping pets or using the local library. On September 1, 1941, the police decree regarding the outward marking or branding of the Jews was passed: from September 15 on, every Jew from the age of six was compelled to wear a yellow star sewn onto his clothes. With this the public humiliation and stigmatization was complete, the surveillance of the persecuted minority perfect. Beginning on July 1, 1943, the Jews in Germany were placed under police control (by the power of decree 13 of the Reich Citizen Law). In other words, there were no longer any legal channels of appeal open to them. By this time, however, there were no longer many Jews living in Germany. Officially, the German Reich was *judenfrei* (free of Jews). A small number had escaped by illegal means, others lived in the dubious safety of Mischehen with non-Jewish partners, prepared at all times for the possibility that they might have to share the fate of the majority of German Jews.

6. GHETTOS IN OCCUPIED EASTERN EUROPE:
The Beginning of the Final Solution of the Jewish Question

At dawn on September 1, 1939, the German army invaded the neighboring country of Poland. The Polish army and air force could offer little resistance to the splendidly equipped Germans: fighting near the border lasted three days, then the advance on Warsaw began. The Polish capital was the target of the first massive air raid of the Second World War. There were many fires throughout Warsaw. Whoever could fled the air raids on the beleaguered city.

The German invasion of Poland was accompanied by antisemitic excesses in which soldiers, ethnic Germans and Poles alike, took part. One Jewish woman from Lodz reported:

"Jew!" We keep hearing this loud cry from the mouths of Germans who until yesterday used to be our neighbors. The wolf has shed his lambskin and he craves prey. German youths lie in wait for passing Jews. They attack them mercilessly, pull at their beards and hair until blood flows, all the while beaming with sadistic pleasure at their wild sport. This has become their "national mission," and they carry it out with proverbial Germany thoroughness. One of our neighbors was taken away for forced labor in the central administration building. After he had scrubbed the floor he was ordered to dry the tiles with his own coat. . . . Only when his clothes were thoroughly soaked with the filthy water was he allowed to get up. Then they shaved off all the hair from part of his head and pushed him out onto the street.

But that was only the beginning. On September 21, 1939, Reinhard Heydrich, chief of the Gestapo and the Security Police, issued instructions to the leaders of the Einsatzgruppen in occupied Poland containing the stages and methods of the Final Solution of the Jewish question:

The planned measures demand the most thorough preparation, in regard to both technical and economic matters. . . . The first step in achieving our final aim is the concentration of the Jews from country areas into the larger cities. This must be carried out without delay. . . . In doing so bear in mind that only those cities that lie at the junction of railway lines or at least on a railway line are to be selected as points of concentration. . . . In every Jewish community a Jewish Council of Elders is to be established, which, as far as possible, should be made up of the remaining influential community figures and rabbis. . . . This council will in fact be held solely responsible for the carrying out of all existing or future instructions, precisely and on schedule. . . . The Jewish councils are to conduct a temporary census of all the Jews—if possible according to gender . . . and the main professional groups—in their local districts and should register the data collected within as short a time as possible. . . . In the general interest of the work of the security police the concentration of the Jews within the cities will necessitate regulations in these cities that make certain districts off limits to Jews, that—and here economic necessity must always be taken into account—for example, forbid Jews to leave the ghetto, or at least forbid them to go out after a certain time in the evening, etc.

Ghettos as places of forced residence designed to humiliate and exploit the Jews were set up under German occupation across Eastern Europe. In the first instance their purpose was to concentrate the Jewish population within the larger cities; the ghettos served as relay stations for the transfer of a huge population, a transfer that lacked any clear structure at the beginning of the occupational rule of Poland. This is clearly demonstrated by the quarreling that went on between the governor general in Cracow and the authorities in the "incorporated districts" of West Poland. For the purpose of "becoming part of the German Reich" the latter wished to be rid of their Jews as soon as possible. Those in power within the Government General, however, also had their sights on a land free of Jews as a long-term goal.

Before the invasion of the Germans there were approximately 350,000 Jews living in Warsaw. After New York they constituted the second largest Jewish community in the world. The majority of Warsaw Jews lived in the north of the city, in the traditionally Jewish quarter, in which Yiddish was spoken. Many of them were Orthodox, dressed completely in black; the men had beards and side curls. Almost half of all the Warsaw Jews worked as tradesmen or manual laborers, a third were in business or commerce. Few were self-employed. Apart from those who were teachers there were hardly any Jews working within the public service. The majority of Polish Jews were poor, and Polish antisemitism had ensured that life before the Germany occupation was not easy. But far worse was to come. First ghettoization and the loss of property. In November 1939 the Germans had appointed the community leader Adam Czerniakow as head of the Jewish Council in Warsaw. In this capacity he was now responsible for a growing number of people who had been evacuated to Warsaw from the surrounding districts. He had to ensure that they were fed, their accommodation and health needs seen to, and he had to carry out orders from the ss that were directed against the Jews.

Czerniakow's diary entries were laconic, often only single words or abbreviations. Nevertheless, they form a record of the day-to-day existence within the Warsaw ghetto:

The statistics for the Jews in Warsaw are complete. 8 A.M. community—contribution. 11 A.M. I take 40,000 zloty in cash to the ss and transfers to the amount of 260,000 zloty. Then to the currency exchange office for the authorization. Signs with the words "Beware! Danger of Contamination. No Entry" will lead to the "ghetto." At the side the commanding officer will put up posters that state that soldiers are forbidden to enter. In the community the collections continue.

The collections were for a contribution imposed on the Jews by the ss, arbitrarily and accompanied by the threat that hostages would be shot if the money was not delivered on time. In a variety of government departments Czerniakow spent his time at meetings urging the administration to find accommodation for the homeless, to allocate funds for the Jewish orphanage, the hospital, and for those in the employ of the Jewish community. The Jewish forced laborers demanded by the Germans had to be recruited. The recruitment was an awful task, arduous and thankless in the extreme.

In the middle of November 1940 the ghetto was sealed off from the outside world with walls and barbed wire. More than four hundred thousand Jews, herded together into a very confined area within the Warsaw ghetto, were living under the control of the Jewish Council, which for its part received its orders directly from the ss.

The position of *Judenältester* at the head of such a *Zwangsgemeinschaft*—enforced community—was a hopeless one. He was constantly humiliated by the ss, arrested and maltreated on a number of occasions, but this did not earn him the love of the ghetto inmates. On the contrary; he was a highly controversial figure. Many regarded him merely as a willing tool of the Germans. This presumption was supported by the most outrageous rumors. The general reprobation Czerniakow earned for having supposedly striven after this difficult post out of vanity and the desire for power to satisfy his own ambition he shared with all those who had been placed by the Germans in positions of authority in the ghettos of Lodz, Vilnius, Lublin, Riga, and Theresienstadt and who, too, like Czerniakow, were mistreated as henchmen. There was no fame after death for members of the Jewish councils, they fared badly at the hands of survivors as well as those who write history, even if they were murdered by the leaders of the National Socialist master race. Their critics, in general, refused to acknowledge the tragic conflict that they embodied.

Adam Czerniakow was an educated and sensitive man.

47

Before World War I he had obtained an engineering degree at the Technical University in his native city of Warsaw and had gone on to study economics there. In Dresden he learned German and immersed himself in German culture. Rampant antisemitism in Poland denied him an office or post outside the Jewish community. That being the case, the man, who by virtue of his background and education felt himself more a Polish patriot than a conscious Jew, took on duties within the Warsaw Jewish community as a teacher at the Technical College and as an association functionary within the Zentrale der jüdischen Handwerker in Polen (Central Office of Jewish Tradesmen in Poland). For some years he was a member of the City Council. In his personal memoirs a comrade-in-arms from the ghetto, Ludwik Hirszfeld, sought to portray the president of the Warsaw Jewish Council fairly:

He liked to present himself as a hard man, yet he possessed the sensitivity of someone who knows that his fate is sealed and who sacrified himself voluntarily. He fought to the end. . . . He had no sympathy with himself. . . . For the lives of those entrusted to his care, however, he fought like a lion. He was courageous in matters relating to his own person, but he was gentle and compliant where others were concerned. He responded, obediently, to the orders of the German authorities and handed over valuables, money, furs . . . even silver chamber pots. When, however, the authorities demanded the people who were in his care, he preferred to sacrifice himself.

In July 1942 the deportation of the ghetto inmates for the extermination camps began. The Jewish councils were, once again, forced to act as henchmen: to draw up the transport lists and to guarantee the readiness to leave of the candidates for death. Even the workers in the ghetto factories who were employed within the German armaments industries were not spared. Czerniakow withdrew from any further henchman's duties for the murderers: on July 23, 1942, he found his escape in suicide. He took poison in his office. A letter to his wife was found on his desk containing only the following: "They are demanding that I kill with my own hands the children of my people. There is no other way out but to die."

Lodz was a flourishing city in Poland, the second largest in the country. Industrial development had favored this city, which boasted above all a significant textile industry. On the eve of World War II Lodz had some seven hundred thousand inhabitants. More than one-third of its citizens were Jews. Lodz was the center of Jewish culture, with Hebrew secondary schools, rabbinical colleges, Yiddish newspapers, many synagogues, and a rich religious life. On September 8, 1939, the city fell into the hands of the German army. Together with the surrounding province, Lodz was annexed to the Warthegau, to become from the end of 1939 onward an integral part of the German Reich. On April 11, 1940, Lodz received a new name, Litzmannstadt, after a German general.

The persecution of the Jews commenced immediately following the German occupation. An SS-Einsatzkommando, supported by local "ethnic German" units, harassed Jewish citizens and looted their property. Forced labor and curfews were the first official measures taken against the Jews. These were followed by exclusion from economic life, the closure of bank accounts, arbitrary arrests. In November 1939 all synagogues throughout the city were destroyed, just as they had been a year earlier in Germany on Reichskristallnacht. Beginning in November 1939 all Jews were forced to wear a distinguishing mark, first a yellow armband, than a Jewish star sewn onto their clothes at chest level.

On December 10, 1940, the *Regierungspräsident* in Kalisch, Friedrich Uebelhoer, as the highest German authority, ordered the preparation of a ghetto:

Following the recruitment of sufficient guards, the ghetto is to be set up in all haste on a day designated by me. That is to say, at an appointed hour the guard units specifically selected for this purpose will take up their positions along the predetermined boundaries of the ghetto. The streets will be closed off by Spanish barbed wire barricades and other barriers. At the same time, the walling up or the sealing off of house facades by other means is to be carried out by Jewish laborers taken from the ghetto. In the ghetto itself a Jewish self-administrative body is to be established immediately, consisting of the Jewish elders and a much enlarged community executive.

On October 13, 1939, Mordechai Chaim Rumkowski had been nominated as Judenältester. In accordance with the orders issued, he had formed the Jewish Council, made up of thirty-one members. On November 11 they were arrested, deported, and murdered. Rumkowski himself was ill-treated and then forced to establish a new Jewish council. There was method in the brutality of the German rulers. First one hundred thousand Jews and two hundred thousand Poles were to leave the Warthegau. The "Jewish question" was to be solved later, once and for all. In a decree issued by Regierungspräsident Uebelhoer the message was very clear: "The establishment of the ghetto is, of course, only a temporary measure. I reserve the right to determine on which days and with what means the ghetto, and as such the city of Lodsch [sic], will be cleansed of Jews. In any event it must be our ultimate goal to completely eradicate this plague spot."

This was in agreement with the planning taking place in Berlin. The Jews from the Warthegau should be deported to the East, to the General Government. However, in January 1940 Hitler's governor in occupied Poland, Hans Frank, refused to accept any more Jews, which in turn intensified the process of ghettoization. The establishment of the Lodz ghetto did not take place as quickly as hoped. The trap did not snap tightly shut, but closed only gradually. On February 8, 1940, the police president ordered the setting up of a ghetto district in the northern suburbs of Lodz, squalid residential areas in which some

62,000 Jews were already living. The ghetto would cover an area of four square kilometers, including the Jewish cemetery, and would comprise 31,000 poorly built houses, almost none of which had running water or was connected to the sewerage system. Here it was intended that 160,000 people live, hermetically sealed off from the world around them. Rumkowski organized a Jewish "police force," a ghetto post office was established, and factories in the ghetto were designed to serve the German armaments industry. Preparations were concluded some time in April. On April 30 the ghetto was sealed off. Leaving the ghetto was punishable by death. In July 1940 Rumkowski was forced to announce the ban whereby "people living inside the ghetto were stricty forbidden to converse over the barbed wire with anyone outside the ghetto, and particularly along the transit streets."

The ghetto was organized and administered with German thoroughness. Under the leadership of Rumkowski, the Jewish Council was there to carry out orders and was responsible for the regulation of the day-to-day lives of the Jews. Within the city administration of Litzmannstadt an Ernährungs- und Wirtschaftsstelle Ghetto (Ghetto office for nutrition and economy) was set up to oversee ghetto affairs. Onward from October 1940 the office, in which four hundred people were temporarily employed, was known as the Ghetto Administration. In charge was Hans Biebow, who in civilian life had been a wholesaler in Bremen. He was an ambitious man who took his duties very seriously and who, like his colleagues, was acutely aware of the significance of the ghetto within the framework of a "solution to the Jewish question." (In April 1947 he was sentenced to death by a Polish court for assisting in the deportation of three hundred thousand Jews to extermination camps and participating in mass shootings; he was executed in June. Proceedings against his colleagues were concluded in the 1970s in the Federal Republic of Germany.)

The Ghetto Administration was responsible for food supply, industrial production, and resources. Patrolling the ghetto from the outside was a matter for the Municipal Police; inside the ghetto this was left to the Secret State Police (Gestapo) and the Criminal Police (Kripo). The Gestapo, the authority dealing with all political opponents and "enemies" of the Reich, maintained its own office within the boundaries of the ghetto. The Kripo was primarily occupied with the confiscation of assets, officially termed the "fight against smuggling."

Ghettoization had been preceded by expropriation. The greater part of the ghetto inmates' possessions did not accompany them during the "resettlement measures"; they were claimed to be abandoned goods and were confiscated. Beginning in July 1940 the "city-state behind bars" possessed its own currency. But even the ghetto money was deemed to be a form of stolen goods, because, according to the official German definition, "it represented nothing more than a receipt for the Reichmark or other currencies that had been exchanged by the Jews. Should the ghetto ever be dissolved, which was not expected, no one possessing ghetto money would have any right of appeal to the German Reich."

On the inside the ghetto was administered by the dictatorial regime of Rumkowski himself. Forced labor in the textile factories, saddleries, carpentry and metal workshops for the German army was organized according to his plans. There was a Jewish police, a prison, a ghetto court of law, a newspaper that carried announcements from the Jewish Council, a statistics department, and an archives in which life in the ghetto was officially recorded. Battling hunger was a daily experience. Hans Biebow, head of the German Ghetto Administration, was well aware of this when he wrote to the Gestapo in March 1942:

For over a year now food rations have been below those approved for prisoners. No one can claim that, in the long term, the ghetto inmates will remain capable of work on the food rations they are given. . . . Moreover, as a rule the food that comes into the ghetto is of an inferior quality. The rapidly rising death toll provides the clearest evidence for the general state of nutrition here. Looking through the death notices over the last weeks one can note an increase in the number of cases of typhus fever (hunger typhus).

Twenty thousand Jews from the German Reich, beginning in autumn 1941—from Vienna, Prague, and Luxembourg—were transported to the ghetto. Schools were closed to create more space. One man who had been dragged off to the ghetto, the publicist Oskar Singer from Prague, confronted with the reality of ghetto existence, asked the following question:

How long does it take for Europeans to loose their cultural veneer under such conditions? Can one maintain this culture with draconian punishments such as the withdrawal of soup or a bed? How is it possible that human beings are not eaten up by lice, if there is no possibilty to clean, change, or air bed linen, undergarments, and clothes? What is culture anyhow?

In November five thousand Roma arrived from the Burgenland, among them a large number of children. They received even harsher treatment than the Jews. They lived in a special compound for gypsies in the ghetto, separated by a double barbed wire fence. In January 1942 they were murdered in mobile gas vans in the Chelmno extermination camp. The deportation of the Jews from the ghetto began on January 16, 1942. Through a campaign of murder the ghetto was gradually to be completely cleared. It fell to the leaders of the Jewish Council to compile the deportation lists. Deportation led to the gas vans in the extermination camp at Chelmno. By September 1942 seventy thousand ghetto inmates had been murdered there. Those who remained in the ghetto were further exploited as slave laborers for the German army and went hungry. In June

1944 Reichsführer—ss Himmler ordered the ghetto to be liquidated. The deportations began again, first to Chelmno, then, starting in August 1944, to Auschwitz. Some still cherished the hope that they were being sent to work.

At the end of August 1944 Rumkowski, the leader of the Jewish Council, was also deported to Auschwitz with his family. The whole tragedy of the Lodz ghetto is reflected in his fate. Rumkowski had come to his office by chance. At the age of sixty-two, with little education, his life had been entirely unremarkable up until 1939. Before taking charge of the ghetto through the grace of the German occupation forces he had been an unsuccessful businessman, insurance agent, and the director of a Jewish orphanage. He had himself called *Präses* and soon earned the hatred of the unhappy ghetto population. Arnold Mostowicz, a ghetto physician, described him as follows:

He was a simple human being but, without doubt, an alert one. His experience in charity work, for example in the organizing of donations, seemed to have been sufficient for him to slip easily into his new role. It suited him perfectly and compensated him perhaps for the subordinate role he played previously. When he gave a speech—he considered himself a good public speaker—and attracted a large audience, he was transported by a sense of power, perhaps, too, by a sense of responsibility.

For those who saw no sense in the measures he took, nor in his iron-rod tactics of maintaining stability and order as head of the massive Jewish ghetto administration, he was regarded as a collaborator of the Germans and a betrayer of the Jews. For those who despised the slave labor that served the armaments production within the ghetto, he was nothing but a pawn of the Germans. On September 4, 1942, Rumkowski gave a speech in front of assembled ghetto inmates. With the pathos of a man in despair, highly dramatizing himself and his role, he declared:

Yesterday I received the order to deport some twenty thousand Jews from the ghetto. If we do not do it, others will. . . . However, as we do not allow ourselves to be ruled by the thought "How many can be saved and how many lost?" but rather by the thought "How many can be saved?" we, that is, my closest colleagues and I, have come to the conclusion that we must take on the responsibility of carrying out this fateful task, however difficult we might find it. I have to perform this difficult and bloody operation, I have to amputate limbs to save the body! . . . In front of you stands a Jew destroyed. . . . This is indeed the most difficult order that I have had to carry out. I stretch out my broken trembling hands to you and beseech you: place your sacrificial offerings in my hands so that I can avoid any further sacrifices, so that I can save a group of one hundred thousand Jews.

The number of survivors of the Lodz ghetto is estimated at 12,000. The ghetto population had reached its peak with 163,623 inmates on December 1, 1941. Under the leadership of Rumkowski the Lodz ghetto had in fact existed eighteen months longer than the Warsaw ghetto led by the morally more sensitive Adam Czerniakow, who in 1942 had preferred to take his own life than be forced to compile further deportation lists as ordered by the Germans. Of course, no one is really in a position to say whether the longer duration of the Lodz ghetto can in fact be attributed to Rumkowski. The controvery surrounding the Jewish councils has sparked long and bitter debates among the survivors.

To the ghettos in Warsaw, Lodz, and Cracow, Tschenstochau, Radom, Kielce, and in many other locations on Polish soil were added from June 1941 in the wake of the German invasion of the Soviet Union ghettos in East Poland, Lithuania, Estonia and Latvia, Belorussia, and Ukraine, ghettos such as Vilnius and Kaunas/Kovno, Riga, Minsk, and, as one of the last, Lvov (August 1942).

On September 15, 1939, the Wehrmacht marched into Bialystok, a city in northeastern Poland with a population of approximately 120,000, half of whom were Jews. Following the secret agreement of the Hitler-Stalin pact, the region fell within the sphere of influence of the Soviet Union. Consequently Bialystok came under Soviet jurisdiction on September 22, 1939. After the German invasion of the Soviet Union, the city came under Nazi rule on the June 27, 1941. The takeover was accompanied by a massacre of the Jews; an Einsatzkommando murdered 2,000 Jewish citizens and destroyed the large synagogue on the first day. A short time later a further 4,000 Jews fell victim to a killing action outside the city. The scenes from autumn 1939 in West Poland repeated themselves in East Poland, in the Baltic States, in Belorussia and Ukraine.

The district of Bialystok was incorporated into East Prussia on August 15, 1941, and as such became a part of the German Reich. Early August saw the start of the ghettoization of the Jews in Bialystok. Five thousand lived and worked under conditions similiar to those in Lodz, controlled by the Gestapo and under the administration of a Jewish council. As in other ghettos, various Jewish political organizations continued their activities: communists, Zionist groups, and the Bund. Despite their differences, these groups had one thing in common: resistance to the oppressor. From August 1942 on, the resistance fighters in the underground were organized into two main camps, which joined forces as one resistance movement in June 1943. They modeled themselves on the Oneg Shabbos organization in the Warsaw ghetto, which armed itself to wage battle with the Germans and prepared secret archival material for posterity. (The documents from the Emanuel Ringelblum Archives, which were stored in milk cans underground, largely survived the liquidation of the Warsaw ghetto. The archives from the Bialystok ghetto were also saved.)

In February 1943 2,000 Jews were shot dead in an

"operation" and another 10,000 were deported to Treblinka. The final order to liquidate the ghetto was issued in August and the task assigned to ss-Gruppenführer Odilo Globocnik. Between August 16–20 the Jewish fighters resisted the superior forces of the Germans, who deployed tanks and artillery fire against the ghetto. The deportation of 30,000 ghetto inmates to Treblinka and Majdanek began on August 18. Twelve thousand children were deported to Theresienstadt and from there to Auschwitz. One group of resistance fighters consisting of about 150 women and men succeeded in escaping from Bialystok and joined the partisans.

The uprising in the Warsaw ghetto in April 1943 was even more troublesome for the National Socialist rulers. The fighting for houses and streets inflicted heavy losses. Within four days the ss had quelled the Jewish resistance. At the end, when the remaining sections of the ghetto had been bombed or burned down, ss-Brigadeführer Jürgen Stroop noted in his report to Berlin, "There is no longer a Jewish residential area in Warsaw!"

The ghettos represented a stepping-stone on the road to the Holocaust. Despite all the misery and suffering, despite all the tragedies that were enacted in them, they were still not the main venues of mass murder. In the years 1940—1943 they were the waiting rooms of destruction, the antechambers of hell, the stations on the way to camps to which human beings were deported for the express purpose of being murdered.

7. FROM ANTISEMITISM TO GENOCIDE:
The Genesis of the Final Solution

In January 1939 Hitler, claiming to speak as a prophet, made the following proclamation in a speech to the Reichstag: "If international Jewish financiers in and outside Europe should succeed once again in plunging the nations into a world war, then it will not end with a victory for Jewry but rather with the annihilation of the Jewish race in Europe."

Hitler was to make reference to this threat on many occasions during the years that followed. Disregarding all the controversy surrounding the question as to whether the extermination of European Jewry was an integral part of the National Socialist program from the beginning or whether the genocide was the result of the radicalization of the Nazi regime sanctioned by the approval of a very large majority, Hitler's announcement of the annihilation provides a key to understanding the tragedy. In the first place, the threat contains the classical stereotype of antisemitism: the claim to an international Jewish conspiracy. This is then extended to the accusation that the Jews were the instigators of World War 1. Last, it draws on the assertion, which had already been propogated in 1933 (and reiterated in 1939), that the Jews had declared war on Germany. In 1933 then the stage was already set for the boycott measures; in 1939 references were made to what, in the covert language of the Nazi state, was called the Final Solution of the Jewish question.

From spring 1941 at the latest this term served as the official circumscription for the physical destruction of the Jews. This linguistic monstrosity stemmed from the pens and mouths of bureaucrats, constructed from the "Jewish question" metaphor, used widely in public discourse since the nineteenth century (as a not necessarily always pejorative collective term for a political, cultural, and social problem area), the "solution" to which, according to antisemites and, of course, then by extension to National Socialist ideology, always lay in exclusion. In the face of the increasing power of the Nazi regime, this idea took on more radical forms.

If the "solution of the Jewish question" was genuinely a postulate of the antisemites and a metaphor of National Socialist propaganda, the real substance of which was still undetermined, the phrase took on a concrete form from 1933 on in the form of measures to strip the Jews of their civil rights, to ostracize them, discriminate against them, and expel them (illustrated most clearly by the Nuremberg Laws of 1935 and their subsequent regulations). It then underwent an intensification to become the "final solution of the Jewish question," which was synonomous with the mass murder of all Jews living within the German sphere of power.

Following the November pogrom of 1938, which marks a transition in the treatment of the Jews from harassment and humiliation to expulsion and destruction, the concept was expanded in official usage to "comprehensive solution" or to the "ultimate" solution of the Jewish question. This semantic radicalization however did not correspond to a clearly defined content, which could more accurately have been described by the term *Sonderbehandlung* (special treatment) in all its unambiguity. The document central to the understanding of the development of this language usage is the "letter of appointment" with which Göring, as Reichsmarschall, plenipotentiary for the Four-Year Plan, and chairman of the Ministerial Office for the Defense of the Reich, authorized on July 31, 1941, the head of the Security Police and the SD Heydrich to make plans:

Following on the decree of 24.1.39, by which you were authorized to find a solution to the Jewish question through emigration or evacuation, a solution most favorable given the particular time frame, I assign you now the task of making all the necessary organizational, practical, and material preparations for a total solution of the Jewish question within the German sphere of influence in Europe. If in doing so you cross into the areas of jurisdiction of other central bodies, then their cooperation should be sought. I further instruct you to present me in the near future with a complete outline of the organizational, practical, and material preliminary measures to be undertaken to achieve the planned final solution of the Jewish question.

The wording of this document is in no way unambiguous with regard to the goals to be pursued; the very reference to the decree of January 1939, which had had the express aim of expiating Jewish emigration, could lend weight to the supposition that the idea behind the "comprehensive solution" was in fact an extension of the pressure for individual emigration: relocation through mass deportations followed by resettlement of the deportees. Whether resettlement really was being discussed at this point in time or whether the decision to commit genocide had indeed already been made has, among historians, long been a subject for debate. The fact that, following the invasion of the Soviet Union (June 22, 1941), the killing commandos of the Einsatzgruppen set about their work in the Baltic states, in Ukraine, in Belorussia, and in Russia well prepared is irrefutable evidence. Official files from this period also include documentary evidence pointing to a shift in meaning of the Final Solution concept that had already taken place. Accordingly, an order issued by the Reich Security Main Office (RSHA), sent as a circular letter on May 20, 1941, to all State Police Headquarters and then as a communiqué to all SD Main Sectors, contains two express references to "the final solution of the Jewish question, which they were undoubtedly approaching." This could only mean an escalation of the Jewish policy as it had been carried out to date. The announcement is also extremely interesting from the point of view that what prompted the order was the lodging of applications by Jews living in Belgium and France for certificates and documents such as police records, passports, etc. These were papers required for emigration overseas. The offices subordinate to the RSHA were advised not to comply with such requests. In more general terms, it was further stated in the RSHA order: "Any migration of Jews to the districts occupied by us is to be avoided, in view of the surely imminent solution of the Jewish question." What possible other purpose could there have been in preventing the emigration of the Jews than the desire to keep them within the German sphere of power in order to hold total sway over them, in other words, to destroy them?

If one can assume with considerable certainty that the term *Final Solution* meant in fact nothing else but annihilation from spring 1941 onward at the latest, then the question must be asked as to when exactly the shift in meaning came about. On June 24, 1940, Heydrich wrote a letter to Foreign Minister Ribbentrop in which he made reference to his responsibility for "ensuring Jewish emigration from the whole Reich territory" (Heydrich referred to Göring's order of January 1939 and made it extremely clear that in the event of discussions in the Foreign Office on the topic of the Final Solution he must be in attendance.) Since January 1, 1939, he went on to state, a total of two hundred thousand Jews had emigrated from Reich territory. Nevertheless, "The entire problem—we are already dealing with around 3 1/4 million Jews in the territories subordinate at this time to German sovereign power—can no longer be solved through emigration. This makes a territorial final solution absolutely necessary."

By a "territorial final solution" the chief of the Reich

Security Main Office meant the Madagaskar-Projekt (Madagascar project), which had been the object of some planning since spring 1940. The idea of settling Jews on the French island colony off the coast of Africa where the climate would be murderous for Europeans can be found in antisemitic literature as far back as the nineteenth century. During the interwar years it was discussed by British writers and in 1937 became the object of French and Polish negotiations. The upshot was a Polish commission that went to the island to examine possible settlement arrangements for Jews from Poland. It is fair to assume that the examination of the situation by the Poles was undertaken more or less seriously. In the opinion of one member of the commission, Lepecki, between forty and sixty thousand people at best could be settled in the Madagascan highlands. Another member, Leon Alter, believed, on the other hand, that at the very most two thousand Jews could be settled on the island.

From time to time the German public was confronted with Madagascan plans. Julius Streicher, an antisemite of the worst sort, propagated a similiar deportation project again in January 1938:

When the *Stürmer* [an antisemitic Nazi newspaper] stated a few years ago that moving the Jews to the French island colony of Madagascar represented a possible solution of the Jewish question, we were mocked by Jews and friends of the Jews and declared inhuman. Today our proposal has become a part of the thinking of foreign statesmen. The daily press reported that at talks held by the French foreign minister Delbos in Warsaw the Jewish question, which is oppressing the Polish people greatly, was discussed. I believe there was talk of diverting a part of the Jewish excess from Poland to Madagascar. However that may be: the new Germany is on a course that leads to deliverance. And beyond a Germany that has been delivered, the world will be delivered. Delivered from the eternal Jew.

The Madagascar plan was in no way a philanthropic project. That was made clear in a speech that the chief ideologue of the Nazi party, Alfred Rosenberg, made in front of representatives from the foreign press and diplomats on February 7, 1939. In it he developed the "idea of solving the Jewish question by establishing a Jewish reserve on Madagascar or in Guyana," after he provided detailed reasons why Palestine did not come into question "for a farsighted emigration policy" and could be just as undesirable as the individual emigration of Jews to all corners of the earth. Apart from the fact that Rosenberg's sympathies quite clearly lay with the Arabs, he considered a Zionist state to be undesirable and dangerous, as it would represent a "totally Jewish center of power in the Middle East," which would serve as an operational base for the worldwide Jewish craving for domination.

Therefore, as Palestine too does not come into question as a solution for a really compact settlement of Jewry, and a dispersed emigration not only does not solve the problem but in racial and political terms conjures up dangers of the very worst kind for Europe and other countries, then the only question that still remains to be resolved is whether the democracies wish to make available a large and self-contained territory, and if so which territory would accommodate the settlement of the entire Jewish people. This territory would have to provide for a capacity of around fifteen million Jews.

From the very beginning the idea of herding the Jews together into ghettos at a remote location contained fantasies of extermination. It was not coincidental that the Jews were intended for districts "at the ends of the earth," where it was hoped that the tropical climate would decimate their numbers, if not eradicate them altogether. So it was then that, apart from Madagascar, Guyana was also considered from time to time. Alaska, as an icy and totally unpopulated wilderness, was also suggested as a Jewish reserve. As far back as the nineteenth century an antisemitic author by the name of Karl Paasch had proposed another penal colony as a variant on murder. The simplest and most practical solution to the Jewish question was extermination. As this did not really seem possible and workable in Germany, he recommended the next best thing: to deport the Jews to New Guinea. This proposal was published in Danzig in 1892 in the *Antisemitenspiegel*.

In 1940 the Madagascar project was pursued for some weeks in earnest. After the German victory over France, and in light of what was believed to be the imminent sub-

mission of England, a Foreign Office official, Franz
Rademacher (the head of D III, the so-called Jewish desk),
began planning how the island of Madagascar, which was
in the process of ceding from France, could be set up as a
Jewish ghetto under German sovereign power. If settlement projects, which in reality were nothing more than
deportation plans, were spurred on by the prospect of
securing colonial territories, it was also evident by spring
1940 that half-hearted attempts to establish a Jewish
reserve in the district of Lublin within the General Government had failed for organizational reasons. In addition
to the technical problems there was also the resistance of
the governor of occupied Poland, Governor General Hans
Frank, who was firm in his stance against deporting the
Jews to his sovereign territory. On July 12, 1940, he
announced to his department heads in Cracow:

Of great importance too is the Führer's decision, made after my
submission, that there should be no more transports of Jews into
the General Government. In general political terms I would like
to add that plans are being made to transport the entire Jewish
tribe in Germany, in the General Government as well as in the
Protectorate to an African or American colony within the short-
est conceivable time after the peace agreement. Madagascar is
being considered and is to cede from France for this purpose.

Hans Frank most strongly opposed the evacuation of
Jews from the annexed territories in Western Poland to the

General Government. Göring was also against such deportations for economic reasons. Heinrich Himmler, as chief of the ss and Reichskommissar für die Festigung deutschen Volkstums (Reich Commissioner for the Strengthening of German Nationhood), responsible for population transfer according to racial politics, noted in his notorious piece of writing "Concerning the Treatment of Foreign Peoples in the East": "I hope to see the concept Jew totally extinguished through the possibility of a mass emigration of all Jews to Africa or to a colony."

Under the leadership of the Foreign Office official Rademacher the Madagascar plan took on a concrete form within the Foreign Office. In June 1940 the mind games included a) the deportation of all Jews from Europe, b) a possible separation of Western and Eastern Jews, whereby the the Eastern Jews would remain "as security in German hands (Lublin?), in order to paralyze the American Jews," while the Western Jews would be deported to Madagascar. Of course, the actual planning was done in the Reich Security Main Office. Heydrich, who on June 24, 1940, had made it unambiguously clear to Ribbentrop that the Final Solution of the Jewish question was his responsibility, commissioned the head of Section IV B 4, Adolf Eichmann, with working out the details. On August 15, 1940, the Foreign Office received the final project description, in which it was remarked in the introduction that the solution to the Jewish problem in Reich territory (including the Protectorate of Bohemia and Moravia) "could scarcely be concluded in the foreseeable future" through emigration because of all manner of difficulties that had arisen. Following the "influx of the masses from the East," it was claimed, "a settlement of the Jewish problem through emigration was impossible." Four million Jews from the German sphere of power were for that reason to be settled in Madagascar, since "an oversees solution to a territory of an insular nature was preferable to any other, to avoid the ongoing contact of other nations with Jews."

The Madagascar plan for the establishment of "a Jewish place of residence under German rule," which, in the opinion of its inventors, would have been "set up internally as a police state," a large de facto ghetto that in character resembled a concentration camp, is the decisive step from the idea of expelling the Jews to that of annihilating them. And the plan already contains all the elements of the later practice of deportation and extermination: the forced cooperation of Jewish organizations with the transports, the theft of all Jewish property before the deportations— registration of property and its utilization), transport under catastrophic conditions. Each person was to be allowed only 200 kg of "nonbulky" luggage. It was intended that two ship transports daily, each carrying 1,500 people, would, as there were 120 ships and the journey lasted 60 days, deport a million Jews each year. With an envisaged total number of 4 million, the project would then be concluded in four years. It was to be financed in part by a contribution imposed on "Jewry resident in the Western powers on the occasion of the peace agreement, as compensation for the damage caused by the Jews to the German Reich in economic as well as other terms following on the Treaty of Versailles." It was hoped that Germany would secure space on ships within the general framework of the peace agreement with England and France into which a relevant clause would be adopted "for the purpose of solving the Jewish problem."

Because a fundamental condition of the Madagascar plan—victory over Great Britain—was not fulfilled, it was discarded soon after its completion in August 1940. For some time the plan did service in the proganda and German foreign policy as the phantom of a supposedly more humane policy toward the Jews. Among other things, this helped conceal the actual intentions. Rademacher, who in the meantime had been promoted to the position of Foreign Office counsellor, closed the file on the Madagascar project in February 1942, shortly after the Wannsee Conference. He wrote to the Africa consultant in the politics section within the Foreign Office, Envoy Bielfeld:

In August 1940 I handed over to you for your files the plan worked out by my section (Jewish desk) for a final solution of the Jewish question. According to this plan, the island of Madagascar was to be demanded from France as part of the peace agreement. The practical implementation of the task was to be left to the Reich Security Main Office. In keeping with the plan, Gruppenführer Heydrich was instructed by the Führer to implement the solution of the Jewish question in Europe. In the meantime, the war against the Soviet Union has presented the possibility of making other territories available for the final solution. Accordingly, the Führer decided that the Jews should not be evacuated to Madagascar but rather to the East. Madagascar then need no longer be designated for the final solution.

If the Madagascar plan can be characterized as a model for extermination, in which the term *Final Solution* is used in its now definitive meaning, it still lacks the ultimate evidence of genocidal intentions because of the exotic and unreal nature of the location and the hypothetical planning. A little-known document from December 1940, a compilation of writings with the title "The Jewish Question," provides us with a clearer indication of the intentions as well as the dimensions that were included in the plans. In notes, which it appears were put together on the occasion of a lecture in the presence of Reichsführer ss Himmler, there are numbers that refer to the movements of the Jewish people (emigration from the Altreich, Germany within the borders of 1937, from the Ostmark, Austria, from the Protectorate, and the "evacuations" from the territories of Western Poland). At an international level the "Jewish question" is clearly and unambiguously divided into two phases: an "initial solution of the Jewish question through emigration (by shifting the initiative from the Jewish political organizations to the Security Police and the sd)" and "the final solution of the Jewish question."

Under this rubric it is stated laconically: "Through resettlement of the Jews from the European economic sphere of the German people to a territory still to be determined. Within the framework of the project about 5.8 million Jews come in to question."

If the radicalization of Jewish policy from deportation to extermination had already begun, all that was missing were the possibilities to carry it out. With the invasion of the Soviet Union in June 1941 the preconditions for implementation, long desired by the the planners of genocide, were suddenly fulfilled.

8. MASSACRE IN THE EAST:
Einsatzgruppen and Other Killing Units in the Occupied Territories, 1941–1942

From the very beginning of the Russian campaign (June 1941), a part of the machinery of destruction already existed in the form of the Einsatzgruppen of the Security Police and the sD. At the same time, deportation of the Jews was being planned or prepared from Germany as well as from the annexed territories and adjacent countries: Austria and the incorporated eastern regions, the Protectorate of Bohemia and Moravia and the General Government (Poland), then the occupied regions of Western and Northern Europe, and, finally, Southern and South Eastern Europe. The Einsatzgruppen were units under the command of the Reichsführer ss Heinrich Himmler, which, as set out in an order from spring 1941, had the right "to carry out of their own accord executionary measures toward the civilian population within the framework of their given task." This was to be understood quite literally, since the Einsatzgruppen had the task of executing *weltanschauliche Gegner* (opponents of the Reich by virtue of their differing worldview, in other words, functionaries of the Communist Party of the Soviet Union), Jews who had positions within the party or state, and other "radical elements." This had been put to the test not only during the Polish campaign but even following upon the annexation of Austria and the invasion of Czechoslovakia, when Einsatzcommandos of the Security Police liquidated potential opponents such as intellectuals, religious leaders, politicians, etc. From summer 1941, from the beginning of the Russian campaign, the Einsatzgruppen—four units comprising a total of three thousand men—functioned as killing commandos that conducted massacres in the Baltic states (Einsatzgruppe A), in Belorussia (B), in Ukraine (C), and in the Crimea (D) of unimaginable proportions. Between June 1941 and April 1942 almost 560,000 human beings were murdered by the Einsatzgruppen, among them virtually the entire Jewish civilian population of the occupied territories. Men, women, and children were driven into forests or onto open fields, shot, and buried in mass graves.

In National Socialist terms the Einsatzgruppen were an elite troop commissioned with the task of pursuing Nazi ideological aims. A large percentage of the positions of leadership within the killing units were occupied by highly educated professionals. Dr. Stahlecker, chief of Einsatzgruppe A, which was responsible for the murder of 229,052 human beings over a nine-month period (according to the "Ereignismeldungen UdSSR"—events reports from the Soviet Union—from the RSHA), was SS and police major general. Among his top-ranking staff were eleven lawyers (nine of them with doctorates). Recruits for the Einsatzgruppen came from the ranks of the Security Police (Gestapo and Criminal Police), the Security Sevice of the Reichsführer SS (SD), and the Waffen-SS. In addition, there were civilian personnel (e.g., translators) who had been drafted for essential services. In their "operations" the Einsatzgruppen were also supported by the indigenous Auxiliary Police, who were recruited from Latvia and Lithuania, Ukraine and Belorussia and who worked alongside the Einsatzgruppen in their murderous campaigns under the name of *Schutzmannschaften*.

One of the tactics of the Einsatzgruppen was to provoke pogroms against the Jewish population, with the help of the indigenous militia and taking advantage of prevailing antisemitic sentiments. In Kaunas/Kovno, then the capital of Lithuania, the following events were recorded immediately following the German invasion at the end of June 1941: "More than 1,500 Jews have been liquidated by

Lithuanian partisans, several synagogues have been set ablaze or destroyed by other means, and a Jewish residential area with about 60 houses burned down." This report was sent by Dr. Stahlecker.

In Libau, the second largest city in Latvia, 2,731 Jewish men, women, and children were murdered in a number of isolated "executions" in front of interested and supportive spectators—among them many soldiers and officers of the German army—between July 1941 and the end of December 1942.

In Bjelaja-Zerkow, 70 km from Kiev, several hundred Jewish men and women were shot by a unit of the Waffen-ss and the Ukrainian militia in August 1941. A short time later their children too were transported on trucks to an execution site and murdered. About ninety children, ranging in age from a few months to five or six years old, were left behind in wretched living conditions, without food and water and guarded by the Ukrainian self-defense militia. Upon the intervention of two military chaplains, the army stepped into action in an attempt to find a solution to the problem.

Lieutenant-Colonel Groscurth reported to the commander-in-chief of the Sixth Army, General Field Marshall von Reichenau, about the events in Bjelaja-Zerkow and established that the troops had been trained to act in an upstanding soldierly manner, "to avoid all forms of violence and brutality toward a defenseless population." The execution of women and children is no worse than the atrocities of the enemy. After such disapproval of the action, the officer, of course, came to the conclusion that "an unavoidable result of the killing by execution commandos of the entire Jewish population of the city was the need to dispose of the Jewish children, particularly the babies. This should have occurred simultaneously with the disposal of the parents to avoid this inhuman torment." General Reichenau's reaction to the report was one of displeasure. He found it impertinent to compare the actions of the German measures with the "atrocities of the enemy" and to include the remark in an open letter. In his opinion "it would have been better not to have written the report at all." A short time later the children were executed. The commander of the ss unit that was given the order to shoot, out of respect for the feelings of his men, suggested that the murders be carried out by Ukrainians. And that is what happened.

The "spontaneous" pogroms, the staged murders for all to see, were followed by systematic executions. The largest massacre took place in Kiev. Apart from the sheer scale of this act of murder it was typical for German operations in the East. In the Baltic states and in Belorussia, in Ukraine and in Russia Jews were "liquidated" in the same way as in Kiev.

On September 28, 1941, the residents of Kiev could read public notices in which all the Jews of the city and its surrounds were asked in Russian, Ukrainian, and German to assemble on the following day for the purpose of resettlement. "You are requested to bring documents, money, valuables, as well as warm clothing, linen, etc. Any Jew who fails to obey this order and is found at a different location will be shot on the spot." The designated meeting place was an intersection close to a goods station, the specified time was 8 o'clock in the morning. Indeed it looked in every way like an evacuation. What the plans really were can be discovered by reading files in the killing headquarters in Berlin. In file number 97 of the report series "Ereignismeldungen UdSSR" (Events Reports from the Soviet Union) it is stated: "According to reports there are 150,000 Jews present. It is not yet possible to verify this information. During the first action, 1,600 arrests, measures underway to take control of the entire Jewish population, the execution of at least 50,000 Jews envisaged. The army welcomes the measures and requests radical action."

German troops marched into the Ukrainian capital of Kiev in September 1941. On the heels of the army was the Sonderkommando 4a from Einsatzgruppe C. The army took part in the events of the following days, if not in the murders themselves, at least in the measures taken to seal off and secure the killing sites. When it was over, engineer soldiers helped to remove all trace of the crimes. The taking by surprise of the Kiev Jews exceeded all expectations. They believed that they were to be evacuated by train to an area deep within the Soviet Union and wanted to be at the designated assembly point early to secure good seats on the transport. The murderers themselves had not reckoned with this, as is evident from the ss report: "Although it had

Just after my arrival at the execution site I had to go into the hollow along with others from my unit. It wasn't long before the first Jews were being led down to us along the ravine slopes. The Jews had to lie down against the sides of the hollow facing downward. In the hollow there were three groups of marksmen, with about twelve marksmen all together. At the same time, Jews kept being led down to these groups of executioners. The Jews that followed had to lie down on top of the corpses of the Jews who had just been shot. Each time the marksmen stood behind the Jews and killed them with a shot in the back of the neck. Even today I can still remember the horror of the Jews at the edge of the pit who could for the first time look on the corpses in the pit. Many Jews screamed with shock. You just cannot imagine the strength of nerves that was needed to carry out this dirty work. It was terrible. . . . I had to stay down in the pit the whole morning. For a while I had to shoot time after time and then I was kept busy loading the machine gun cartridges with ammunition. During this time others from the unit were assigned the job as marksmen. At about midday we were pulled out of the pit and in the afternoon I was at the top and had to help lead the Jews to the hollow. During this time there were others down in the hollow doing the shooting. The Jews were led by us as far as the edge of the hollow, then they ran down the slopes alone. The entire shooting on this day might have gone on until . . . 5 or 6 P.M. After that we went back to our quarters. There was alcohol (schnapps) again on this evening.

The murdering went on for two days. The report sent to Berlin, Events Report No. 101, dated October 2, 1941, provides the final death count with military precision: "Sonderkommando 4a, in cooperation with Group Staff and two commandos from Police-Regiment South, executed 33,771 Jews in Kiev on 29. and 30.9.41."

The number of those murdered is as authenticated as the testimonies of perpetrators, onlookers, and a number of survivors. One member of the Sonderkommando, in civilian life a policeman and perhaps, like the other murderers, a good husband and father, friend of animals or club chairman, pleasant neighbor or jovial drinking partner, reported on the events in the style of someone who did no more than perform his duty, who only carried out unavoidable orders:

On the third day after the execution we were driven back to the site of the execution. As we arrived we noticed a woman sitting near a bush who had apparently survived the execution unscathed. This woman was shot by the SD man—name unknown—who was accompanying us. Then we saw a person from the pile of corpses waving their hand. Whether it was a woman or a man, I don't know . . .

I never went back to the site of the execution after this day. After that we were busy for some days smoothing out the bank notes which had come from the property of the Jews that had been shot. I would estimate that we were dealing with an amount in the millions. I don't know what happened to the money. It was packed into sacks and sent away.

Over the following days the corpses were covered with earth. A unit of engineer soldiers from the army was given the task of blowing up the sides of the ravine. In that way an enormous mass grave was created. In the official Events Report of the ss it was stated: "The 'resettlement measure' that was conducted against the Jews met with the full approval of the population. The fact that the Jews were in fact liquidated is scarcely known yet and, based on experiences made up to now, would hardly meet with any disapproval. The measures taken were also welcomed by the army."

The murdering in Babi Yar continued into August 1943. In the final act of this tragedy Jewish concentration camp inmates were forced to exhume the bodies. They were burned in improvised fireplaces, the bone fragments left over in the ashes were crushed and ground to dust. After the withdrawal of the Germans from Ukraine, nothing was to remain that would bear witness to the crimes. Since spring 1943 eradicating all traces of the mass murders in the east had been the special task of Sonderkommando 1005, under the leadership of ss-Colonel Paul Blobel. He had also been chief of the unit charged with the duty of conducting the mass murders in Babi Yar in September 1941. Blobel was sentenced to death in Nuremberg in 1948 and executed in Landsberg in 1951.

The massacres of the Jews had been relatively public events, carried out with the knowledge of the army and the civil occupational authorities and certainly not exclusively by ss-units. On July 13, 1942, in Josefow in Poland members of the Reserve Police Batallion 101 murdered on order 1,500 Jewish men, women, and children by shooting them in the back of the neck. The commander of the batallion had been distraught about the order, while those assigned to carry it out, order police in civilian life, were embittered about the unreasonable demand made of them and depressed. The men grew accustomed to murdering during later massacres, in the district of Lublin, in the course of liquidating ghettos, the *Judenjagd* (the tracking down and killing of Jews in hiding), as well as the large-scale actions in Majdanek and Poniatova. The just under 500 men who at the end of the war returned to their civilian professions—the majority were police officers in Hamburg—had taken part in at least 83,500 murders on Polish territory. (In the 1960s 210 former batallion members were interrogated, 14 indicted, and a small number convicted. The latter received only light sentences.)

The mass murder of Jews did not however take place only in the occupied eastern territories. In Yugoslavia, where from April 1941 on German troops waged war and established an occupational regime (Croatia had become an independent fascist state de jure, Serbia was under German military administration), the path to the Holocaust took a similar course. In 1941 there were seventeen thousand Jews living in Serbia who, under German rule, experienced all the stages of discrimination, withdrawal of civil rights, and the destruction of their economic existence. The difference was that the stages succeeded each other more rapidly. Very little time passed between stigmatization and physical destruction. A year after the German occupation, Serbia was declared judenfrei.

A further distinction from Poland and the other eastern territories was the fact that in Yugoslavia the phase of ghettoization was bypassed and the army played a more active role in the destruction of the Jews. Under the guise of partisan warfare Jews and Romanis were taken as hostages and shot as part of military "reprisal expeditions." The army, the military administration, and the Foreign Office (whose representative in Belgrade was the head of the Jewish Section Rademacher) cooperated in numerous actions in which male Jews and Romanis were shot. On November 1, 1941, Lieutenant Colonel Walther reported on "the shooting of Jews and gypsies" by members of infantry regiment 433:

Most of the time is taken up with digging out the graves, while the shooting itself is very fast (a hundred people every forty minutes). . . . Shooting the Jews is easier than shooting the gypsies. I have to admit that the Jews are very composed as they go to their death—they stand very calmly—while the gypsies wail and scream and move about constantly when they are already standing at the execution site.

The women and children were interned in the concentration camp at Sajmiste. Together with a fairly large number of old men, five hundred men initially recruited as forced laborers, and about three hundred Romani women, there were approximately seventy-five hundred people in the camp. Between March and May 1942 they were murdered in gas vans, on the journey from Sajmiste directly through Belgrade to Jaijnce, where the corpses were unloaded and thrown into pits. The gas vans, which had been brought especially for this purpose from Berlin to Belgrade, were then transported back to Berlin, overhauled, and put into service again in Belorussia (Minsk).

9. THE DEPORTATION OF THE JEWS
FROM GERMANY

The systematic deportation of the Jews from Germany—overseen by bureaucrats and planned down to the finest detail—began in autumn 1941 and represented the final stage of National Socialist policy toward the Jews. The policy now clearly demonstated a single-mindedness in its express and exclusive aim to annihilate the Jews of Europe.

The preparations were carried out with complete thoroughness and were concluded in the middle of October 1941. Jews everywhere received a printed summons to present themselves for "evacuation" at collection points. They had been sent a code of conduct—what they should take with them for "settlement in the East" and in what condition they should leave their apartments (light, gas, and water bills were to be paid before departure). At the same time that they received an "evacuation number" they were informed that their entire property had been confiscated by the state police retrospective to October 15, 1941. In addition, if any part of their estate had been sold or given away since that date, that act was now declared invalid. Every Jew was ordered to draw up a statement of property including all items sold or given away since that time together with the names and addresses of the new owners. This inventory of assets was to be accompanied by numerous relevant documents such as promissory notes, stocks, and shares, insurance policies, purchase agreements, etc.

In this way a precedent was set for the theft of Jewish property, whereby those being robbed were forced into doing the bureaucratic dirty work. Such theft was formally legalized by decree 11 of the Reichsbürgergesetz—the Reich Citizen Law—one of the Nuremberg Laws of 1935. Step by step the rights of the Jews were curtailed through the implementation of numerous decrees until finally all those who had not been able to emigrate in time were herded together into ghettos and death camps. Decree 11, which came into force on November 25, 1941, stipulated under what circumstances the Jews were to be stripped of their German citizenship and set out the details; this loss of citizenship automatically went hand in hand with "the transfer of the usual place of residence abroad." The purpose of this stipulation was made very clear in paragraph 3: With the loss of citizenship the property of the Jews falls to the state. In order to exclude any possibility of circumventing this regulation the section of the RSHA that was responsible for Jewish affairs, in other words, Gestapo headquarters in Berlin, imposed restrictions on the movement of Jewish property. This order, too, dated October 27, 1941, applied retrospectively to October 15, 1941. It was clearly designed to prevent the movement of assets before the deportation of the Jews.

If the legal constructs pertaining to a retrospective loss of citizenship and property were not dubious enough, in addition, "the transfer of the usual place of residence abroad," in fact, was left in no way to the discretion of the Jews themselves. Emigration, which the authorities had made compulsory in the years 1938–1939, was indeed outlawed in autumn 1941. Even given the fact that they were unaware of what would happen to them, those concerned did not aspire to an evacuation. At the beginning of December 1941, by way of closing the last hole in the net designed to ensnare the Jews in order to rob them of their very existence, the Reich Ministry for the Interior set about defining the term *abroad* in the case of deportation within a secret order accompanying the implementation of decree 11 of the Reich's Citizen Law: "The withdrawal of citizenship and the handing over of property applies also to those . . . Jews, whose usual place of residence is now or in the future will be in the territories occupied by German troops or under German administration, especially in the Government General, in the Baltic states, in White Russia and Ukraine."

Through these legislative measures a framework for the expulsion of the Jews from Germany had been established. Indeed, the deportation of the Jews from Reich territory had already been rehearsed at various locations: ghettoization and the expulsion of the Jewish population on a large scale had already directly followed the march into Poland in autumn 1939 with the annexation of territories in the west of the country. Barely six months after the beginning of the war the first German Jews were deported from Pomerania: on February 12, 1940, 1,000 Jews from Stettin and the surrounding districts were taken from their homes at night and transported to three villages close to Lublin. In March 1940 their fate was shared by 360 Jews from the Reich district of Schneidemühl. The action was justified on the grounds of urgent need of living space in the interest of war economy. Only few survived this deportation; most fell victim to the mass murders that began in the spring of 1942.

The initiative for a further action that was carried out in the *Gaue* of Baden and the Saarland Palatinate at the end of October 1940 was provided by the two Nazi gauleiter (highest-ranking party functionaries) Robert Wagner

(Baden) and Josef Bürckel (Saarland Palatinate). Because of personnel sharing these two men were also heads of the civilian administrations in Elsass and Lothringen, providing them with special authority from which they claimed the right to have approximately sixty-five hundred Jews arrested by the Gestapo. These Jews were transported from collection points in major cities by train to the south of France, which was unoccupied by the Germans and where they were interned by the Vichy government, not without some protest from Berlin. Although many perished either during the transport or soon after, about one-third of those deported in the *Bürckel-Aktion* survived. Both the action in Pomerania as well as that in South West Germany had a limited regional scope and for the moment remained isolated events. German Jews were granted a last reprieve. The actions themselves, however, just like the deportations from Austria that followed the Anschluss, must be regarded as test cases for the general deportation of all Jews from the German Reich.

While the ss Einsatzgruppen in the East had long been committing mass murder in grand style against Polish, Ukrainian, and Russian Jews, the Gestapo in the West was now paving the way for deportations. Even before the Wannsee Conference all the necessary machinery was in full swing. Across the Reich the deportations had been organized in the most efficient manner possible. From the beginning of November 1941 approximately one thousand people in each case, under the guard of Order Police, were deported from central locations that served as collection points. They were transported by train, despite the reservations expressed by military quarters, where there was an urgent need for transport facilities. Deportation trains from Berlin, Hamburg, Hanover, Dortmund, Münster, Düsseldorf, Cologne, Frankfurt/Main, Kassel, Stuttgart, Nuremberg, Munich, and Breslau left Reich territory headed for Riga or Minsk. (In November 1941 four trains were diverted to Kaunas/Kovno.) Approximately twenty thousand Jews from the Altreich (Germany within the boundaries of 1937) fell victim to this wave of deportations. A further thirty thousand were deported from the Ostmark (Austria), with Vienna serving as the collection point, and the Reich Protectorate of Bohemia and Moravia, with Prague as the collection point. These transports took place between November 8, 1941, and January 25, 1942. On March 6, 1942, a further series of transports was discussed in the RSHA by Eichmann and representatives of local Gestapo headquarters. From March 1942 fifty-five thousand Jews from the Altreich, from the Ostmark and the Protectorate, among them seventeen thousand from Germany, were transported to the East, in some cases first to transit camps such as Izbica and Piaski, where as internees they were subjected to forced labor, and then on to the extermination camps of Belzec (in the district of Lublin) and Sobibor. Transports to Riga also continued as late as 1942. In the paper work that accompanied the expulsion, which documented de facto the extinguishing of the civil existence of the victims, the place of destination was often given only as the "East." This makes it difficult if not impossible to trace the fate of individuals to their place of murder.

The *Reichsjuden-Ghetto*—ghetto for Jews from within the Reich—in Riga-Skirotava was dissolved on November 2, 1943. It can only be assumed that all those who had been deported there at the end of 1941 fell victim to the mass executions carried out by Einsatzgruppe A. It must also be assumed that those who were brought to Piaski and Izbica found their deaths in the gas chambers of the extermination camps of Belzec and Sobibor. In June 1942 six thousand people were transported from Piaski, 20 kilometers southeast of Lublin, to Trawniki. In November 1942 a transport of an unknown number arrived at the extermination camp of Sobibor, in March/April 1943 the camp was liquidated and the inmates were brought to Trawniki and to the extermination camp of Belzec.

Trawniki was a transit camp in the district of Lublin and was in operation from 1941 to 1943. The internees of Trawniki, who were en route to Izbica, near the Polish city of Krasnystaw in the district of Lublin, seldom spent long periods of time there. After a short stay most were shipped on to the extermination camps—to Belzec, Chelmno, Sobibor, Majdanek, or Treblinka.

The fate of individual deportees can be reconstructed with the help of Gestapo files, which are the most authentic documents available. On November 23, 1941, Martha

"Sara" Handburger, née Engelhardt, testified with her signature that she had been informed by the Secret State Police, State Police Office Nuremberg-Fürth, Würzburg branch, that she would be evacuated on November 27 and her entire property confiscated. The signature appears on a duplicated document under the heading "announcement." The document is officially dated and is complete with the signature of a police inspector. Apart from Martha Handburger's evacuation number 239, which is written in by hand, it contains her last address in Würzburg: Hindenburgstrasse 21.

Three days before their departure the Jews of Würzburg who had been selected for "evacuation" were summoned to a meeting where they were issued a code of conduct for the journey on which they were about to embark, where indeed they were instructed on the final stage of the destruction of what remained of their civic existences.

The instruction sheet that was pressed into Martha Handburger's hand on November 23, 1941, showed clearly how efficient the bureaucratic apparatus was, how detailed the planning and preparations, right down to the transport costs imposed on the victims. Frau Handburger was also instructed about the following details:

With the ration cards that are currently in my possession I am to purchase provisions for a march lasting at least three weeks and for a further four days. I am aware that I have no further claim to rations, in the event of my provisions being consumed before this time. I have also been instructed that I am to bring my suitcase—maximum weight of 50 kg (no bulky items!) to the freight depot at Aumühle between 8 and 10 o'clock on 26.11.1941; in addition, my remaining possessions from the ghetto are to be ready for collection by the Jewish work commando from the 25.11.41. I am to include 60 Reichsmark for the transport costs.

At some time during November 24 everyone selected for deportation was also to hand in all valuables and documents together with the statement of property "in a tough, open envelope" with an exact address and evacuation number. Between that date and November 26, when the unfortunate deportees had to report for "evacuation" in the city hall between 2 and 4 P.M., each still had time to see to his apartment, which meant in effect to leave it in such a way

that following my departure it can be sealed up by the police (gas, light, and water, etc., must be turned off!). I am to remove all perishable goods. The fires in the fireplaces must have been extinguished. I am to leave the apartment clean and tidy; before I leave, the gas and light bills must be paid at the city public works office. I will inform the concierge of my evacuation. All my room and apartment keys are to be attached to a keyring that is clearly labeled with my Würzburg address and that I am to hand over to the Würzburg branch of the State Police on arrival at the city hall.

Among the files of the Würzburg Gestapo can be found the few personal papers that document the end of the civic existences of the married couple Martha and Adolf Handburger: the joint, handwritten statement of property showing that apart from clothing and a modest household the Handburgers possessed 2,788 Reichsmark in the bank and bonds valued at over 1,700 Reichsmark, medical documents relating to an injury that Adolf Handburger had sustained while working for a construction company, a birth certificate, a certificate for training in anti-aircraft defense, and a standard printed letter of notification from the American Consul General in Stuttgart dated April 21, 1941, in which receipt of the application for emigration to the United States was acknowledged. The only personalized part of the document was the registration number 25404, which had been issued to two people. The bearers of this number were identical with the bearers of evacuation numbers 238 and 239 assigned by the Würzburg Gestapo, for whom the file Handburger was closed with an entry "Evacuation to the East" as a result of a decree from the Reichsführer ss. The personal documents that were part of the file "were located and taken possession of on 27.11.1941 when the above mentioned were bodily searched in Nuremburg."

The 202 Würzburg Jews, among them 40 children and teenagers, had gathered punctually on November 26 in the city hall. They had been subjected to very tight controls during which they were forced to hand over a number of their possessions. The Gestapo kept lists of the cameras, knives, scissors, stamps, and other objects that were taken from the Jews. At 4 A.M. on November 27, 1941, the Jews, who had spent the night in the main room of the city hall, were herded together to the station at Aumühle. Four passenger and two goods carriages were waiting for them. These were coupled to a goods train that left Würzburg at 5:50 A.M. and arrived in Nuremberg at 10:36 A.M. The camp at Langwasser was their last stop on German territory. It was here that the final transport was put together. There were 535 Jewish deportees from Nuremberg; on the afternoon of November 27 they were joined by 106 Jews from Bamberg. Members of the Coburg and Bayreuth Jewish communities made up the total of 1,000.

The painstaking search and stripping of belongings went on for hours. In one room the suitcases were searched and prohibited objects (jewelry, money, and many more) confiscated. In the adjoining room personal papers and valuables (which had not been handed in in the owner's hometown) had to be handed over. What was left was a wedding ring, a watch, an identity card. In a third room a humiliating body search was carried out. The Gestapo was at pains to make absolutely sure that nothing was being smuggled out. In a fourth room the loss of property was made official by a writ of summons and identity cards, in a final bureaucratic gesture, were stamped with the word *Evacuated*. Nothing remained to do but await departure, in camp barracks, guarded by ss men and with

Jewish helpers responsible for maintaining order and cleanliness. At 12:30 P.M. on November 29 the train was declared ready for departure, at 3 P.M. it finally pulled out of the station. The destination was Riga, the capital city of Latvia, which, as part of the Reichskommisariat Ostland was now under German administration.

The deported Jews had been led to believe that they were being evacuated for settlement in the East and they for this reason had been asked to bring along certain household items and technical or building equipment. These were loaded on to the train with the help of Jewish volunteers who had been selected by the local Jewish Council. In Würzburg the following were among the items brought to the railway station as "ghetto luggage": fifteen sewing machines, twenty-nine stoves equipped with stove pipes, fifty glass window panes, a set of work tools for a butcher, a cobbler, a precision engineer, a hairdresser, a dressmaker, a men's tailor, building equipment.

The trip to Riga lasted three days and three nights. In addition to the permanent hunger and thirst, the deportees had to endure the torments of the accompanying ss guards. Everyone and everything was offloaded at the station in Skirotava. Exposed to beatings and other forms of maltreatment from German and Latvian ss officers, the Jews were now forced to march to the camp of Jungfernhof, a former goods yard. Everyone was accommodated in barracks and barns. It was icy cold, the sanitary conditions appalling, the food inadequate. Of the five thousand human beings who were living herded together in this way—in addition to the transport from Bavaria, a further two deportation trains from Vienna as well as one from Hamburg and one from Württemberg arrived—between twenty and thirty perished each day. There were so many deaths that finally the corpses had to be burned on funeral pires. It was impossible to bury them because the ground was frozen solid.

For most of the deportees the camp of Jungfernhof or the ghetto in Riga became their final destination. Herbert Mai, one of the few survivors, who as a twelve year old had arrived at Jungfernhof with his parents on the transport of November 27, 1941, reported what took place on March 27:

At 6 o'clock in the morning everyone had to asssemble in the camp square. All those who were to stay there were locked into one of the larger barracks, with men and women separated. My father and I were among them and my mother too. At the time there were 6,000 people in the camp. At this point large sealed buses arrived and the people were loaded on. On this day 5,000 were driven away.

Weeks later those who were left behind learned from local residents and in roundabout ways that everyone who had supposedly been driven to a "work detail"—had been shot dead in a forest near Riga on the same day they left. Einsatzgruppe A bears the burden of responsibility for these mass murders, which, according to civilian reports, resembled assembly line work. Deportees sent to work on the land heard from local farmers that the victims were made to take off their clothes before they stepped onto the footbridges that had been erected over the massive graves. Struck by the bullets of the murderers, they then plunged into the mass grave.

Due to the anonymity that surrounded these events as well as to the fact that the Einsatzgruppen later covered over all traces of their actions, it is in most cases nearly impossible to find evidence pointing to the individual fate of the deportees once they left their hometowns. Only one thing is certain: almost all were murdered in the cruelest of fashions. In a statement made to a Soviet investigating committee in 1944 one female citizen of Riga described events as follows:

My house is situated only one to one and a half kilometers from the forest, so I could see the people being brought to the forest and I could hear them being shot. I know that the Germans once shot more than ten thousand people over a period of two days. That was on the Good Friday and Saturday before Easter in 1942. Each time the people were brought in four or five buses or other vehicles, which arrived at half hourly to hourly intervals. The buses and cars were crammed full of Jews. On both these days—on Friday and Saturday—they came continuously, day and night. On Friday alone I counted forty-one buses bringing people to the forest within a twelve-hour period. About twenty to thirty minutes later they came back out of the forest empty. Day and night other local residents and I could hear the shots from rifles and automatic weapons. The clothes of the people who had been murdered were taken away in the vehicles that returned from the forest.

On Easter Sunday silence fell and this witness, like many other local residents, went into the forest to view the mass graves:

Jews from other countries had also been shot. You could see that from the various objects that had been left behind. Next to just about every grave were the remains of a fire where the fascists had burned useless objects. You could see from the ashes that clothing had been burned, because in the ashes were buttons, buckles, spectacle cases and frames, the metal parts of ladies' handbags, wallets, and purses as well as many personal effects. At the sites of these fires and next to the graves you could find various papers, photographs, and identifying documents. It was possible to work out from the documents and photographs where the people came from, because on the back of the photographs you could make out the name of the photographer and the town. In that way it was possible to learn that the people who had been shot at this spot had been brought here from Austria, Hungary, Germany, and other countries.

Yet another transport from Germany. On November 20, 1941, one thousand human beings left Munich; their destination too was Riga. The collection point for the Jews from throughout Altbayern and Schwaben was in Munich. Camp barracks in Milbertshofen (Knorrstrasse 148), which had been constructed in spring 1941 by Jewish forced laborers on an area of 14,500 square meter, served as a transit and check point for the deportees.

Else Behrend-Rosenfeld was director of the Jewish "hostel"—within the convent of the Sisters of Mercy in the district of Berg am Laim in Munich. It was in fact a type of ghetto for the elderly. In April 1942 she received her notice of deportation. Before being allowed, at the very last minute, to stay, she went through the entire preparations for deportation in Milbertshofen. After being ordered to proceed in single file to the barracks for inspection by the Gestapo, the following scene took place:

Behind a barricade made out of tables a man was sitting who gave the perfunctory order, "Empty your handbag." I emptied the contents of my bag onto the table in front of him. The first thing he grabbed was my identity card and he placed it on the pile of cards he already had. . . . He seized the few photos still in my possession. . . . Damn! He had torn them right down the middle and threw them over his shoulder. . . . He opened my purse, which contained some coins. . . . I set about putting the remaining things back into my handbag, but a gesture from him stopped me. "None of that, move along. Next!" he bellowed.

Between 3,000 and 4,000 Jews were deported via the transit point of Milbertshofen, 2,991 of them from Munich.

The transport to Riga was followed by another on April 3, 1942. This time the destination was Piaski, near Lublin. The deportees included 343 Jews from Munich and 433 from Swabia as well as 213 Jews who had arrived the day before via the collection point in Regensburg. With one exception—a transport to Auschwitz on March 13, 1943—the destination of all the remaining forty deportations from Munich was the ghetto of Theresienstadt.

10. THERESIENSTADT

This North Bohemian town, situated close to the point where the Eger flows into the Elbe, was founded in 1780 by Kaiser Josef II as an Austrian fortress and enjoyed the reputation at the time of being a masterpiece of military architecture. During the 1930s Theresienstadt had a population of somewhat more than 7,000, half of its residents being soldiers. From the end of 1941 onward the small town served as the ghetto for the Jews from the Protectorate of Bohemia and Moravia. At the end of May 1942 a third of them (28,900) found themselves in Theresienstadt. To all intents and purposes a concentration camp, under the command of the ss, guarded from the outside by the Czech gendarmerie (rural police), the town was a transit point and point of transfer for Jewish men, women, and children. The first deportation from Theresienstadt to Riga took place in January 1942. In July 1942 all the original residents of the town were evacuated to make room for transports from Germany, Austria, Denmark, and the Netherlands.

Among the forty thousand German Jews who were transported to Theresienstadt beginning in June 1942 there was the widespread illusion that, as prominent individuals who were being given preferential treatment, they were en route to a ghetto for the privileged only. The cynicisim of the Nazi regime went so far as to engage the help of the Reich Association of Jews in robbing the deportees to Theresienstadt of their entire worldly goods. In *Heimeinkaufsverträge* (contracts to secure a place in a home) they were promised residence in a restful old age home where they would receive medical attention and care in the event of illness.

The first paragraph of the contracts contained the following clause:

As it is the responsibility of the Reich Association of Jews to provide the necessary means for care of the entire population housed communally in Theresienstadt, including those who are in need, it is the duty of all those to be accommodated in this community, with the capital at their disposal, to provide as far as possible the means for care of the needy as well as their own accommodation through contributions paid to the Reich Association of Jews.

104

A signature at the end of this clause indicated that it had been understood and accepted.

The completed contract meant the state had agreed to "guarantee, for the rest of one's life, the cover of board and food expenses in the old age home, to have one's washing done, and, when necessary, to provide medical treatment and medication." However, reserved was "the right to move the accommodation elsewhere" and "in the event of any change in the current accommodation arrangements" the person entering the contract could make no further claims. The German Jews who arrived at Theresienstadt had bought themselves a place in the concentration camp with their own capital. Theresienstadt was under the jurisdiction of the Zentralstelle für jüdische Auswanderung Prag (The Central Office for Jewish Emigration in Prague), a fact that helped maintain the fiction that the Final Solution was really all about resettlement measures. On an order from Heydrich the ghetto was officially established in February 1942 and an ss commando dispatched to take control. Next to the ghetto was the "small fortress," which fell under the jurisdiction of Gestapo headquarters in Prague and was a place of intimidation and torture, with its own commanding officer in charge.

Arrival at Theresienstadt was a shock to the system. Overcrowded mass accommodation in old, decrepit barracks, undernourishment and horrific sanitary conditions awaited those who had expected an old age home. Many of the generally elderly people were unable to cope with the living conditions; they died soon after their arrival at Theresienstadt. The death rate in 1942 was higher than 50 percent, fell in 1943 to 29.4 percent, and in 1944 was 17.2 percent. Many, however, did not fall victim to the external conditions but rather to the extreme insult they had sustained.

For the Jews from the German-speaking realm, for these highly assimilated representatives of German culture, the reality of Theresienstadt became synonymous with their betrayal by the Germans. In 1933 they had still felt secure, believing as they did in Emancipation, because they simply could not imagine that their services to what they had believed was a common fatherland could be ignored, their patriotism trampled on, their affinity with German culture despised, and their citizenship no longer recognized, indeed, made defunct. Since 1933 German Jews had had to endure various forms of discrimination, the purpose of which was to exclude them from German society and ultimately deprived them of their material existence. This was followed by physical annihilation—through hunger, sickness, and despair in the transit camp at Theresienstadt and in other camps, through killing units and in the gas chambers in the East—but not before they had borne the humiliation of seeing Emancipation annulled and being banished to the ghetto.

What was to be the fate of 90 percent of all Jews from Bohemia and Moravia—deportation to the transit camp at Theresienstadt (from where they were later transferred to a more terrible site and their eventual annihilation)—was presented to the German Jews as a privilege. This served a number of purposes. It was intended for one thing that transport to the extermination camps be covered up. For another, the deportation of prominent and privileged German Jews (who were joined later by certain groups of Jews from Denmark and Holland) to a privileged location was designed to prevent possible representations on their behalf. After all, for a small group of German Jews Theresienstadt was indeed a privileged final destination—that is, if they were able to endure the sanitary conditions, the hunger, and the degradation.

A decree from the RSHA dated May 21, 1942, lists the following groups of people from the territory of the German Reich as those intended for the "ghetto for the aged"—as announced by Heydrich at the Wannsee Conference: those over the age of sixty-five, as well as infirm Jews over the age of fifty-five with their spouses, veterans of World War I who were highly decorated or had *Verwundetenabzeichen* (injury insignia), together with their wives, Jewish spouses from no longer existing German-Jewish mixed marriages, and, finally, unmarried Jewish Mischlinge, if they were regarded as Jews under the prevailing regulations.

The deportations of German Jews to Theresienstadt, so-called evacuation transports, began on June 2, 1942. The official end of Jewish life in Germany dates one year later. On the morning of June 10, 1943, the Gestapo arrived in the office of the Berlin Jewish Community Center at 29

Oranienburgerstrasse with the news that the Jüdische Kul-
tusvereinigung zu Berlin—Jewish Cultural Association of
Berlin—(the official title since April 30, 1941) had ceased
to exist. All employees except those living in Mischehen—
mixed marriages—with "Aryans" were arrested, taken to
the assembly camp, Grosse Hamburgerstrasse, and transported on June 16, 1943, to the railway station in Putlitz-
strasse. On that same evening an estimated five hundred
Jewish men, women, and children, among them three hundred who were sick, left the capital of the Reich on a
deportation train. From that point on, Berlin, and with it
Germany, was considered to be judenfrei.

The same fate was also suffered by the five remaining
staff members of the Reichsvereinigung der Juden in
Deutschland (Reich Association of Jews in Germany). Its
sphere of influence had continued to be curtailed. Since
November 1938 the autonomous umbrella organization of
German Jewry, which had been founded in 1933, had been
reduced step by step to an institution whose every action
was determined by the controlling hand and the orders of
the Gestapo. The Reichsvereinigung der Juden in
Deutschland, as the organization had been known since
July 1939, the successor organization of the Reichsvertretung der deutschen Juden (1933)—Reich Agency of German Jews— and the Reichsvertretung der Juden in
Deutschland (1935)—Reich Agency of Jews in Germany— was no longer a voluntary amalgamation of different groups but rather an institution that had come into

existence by force with jurisdiction over all people classified as Jews by the Ariergesetzgebung—so-called Aryan
legislation—irrespective of their religious beliefs. By
decree of the RSHA all existing Jewish organizations and
trusts had lost their independence by being integrated into
the Reichsvereinigung. Finally, on January 29, 1943, the
same fate befell the Jewish community in Berlin. On June
10, 1943, all the district offices of the Reichsvereinigung
outside Berlin were dissolved. Their assets were confiscated
to the benefit of the German state.

Controversy still exists among historians about the sta-
tus of the Reichsvereinigung der Juden in Deutschland in
its final phase. The fact that the Reichsvereinigung became
a pawn in the hands of the Gestapo in the deportation and
destruction of the German Jews cannot be overlooked.
From the middle of 1942 on, the Reichsvereinigung primarily had the duty of delivering the lists, of passing on
orders from the Gestapo, and of keeping statistics on the
deportations. Needless to say, the forced participation of
the Reichsvereinigung in the deportations did not turn it
into a national socialist organization performing its "dirty
work" happily or even in tacit agreement with the Nazi
regime. Even if it appeared to be the case to some of the
victims, the staff members of the Reichsvereinigung never
joined the side of the perpetrators.

Even before the amalgamation, the leadership of the
Reichsvereinigung had been almost identical with that of
the Berlin community. Long before June 10, 1943, they too

had been repeatedly the victims of the deportations. Of the thirteen leading figures, only two survived the persecution: Moritz Henschel, who was transported to Theresienstadt on June 16, 1943, and Rabbi Leo Baeck, who had been deported to Theresienstadt on January 28, 1943. There, as members of the "Council of Jewish Elders," which was responsible for the self-administration of the ghetto, the remains of the former umbrella organization of German Jewry continued to exist until their liberation on May 8, 1945. They were represented by such prominent figures as Leo Baeck, Paul Eppstein, Moritz Henschel, Philipp Kozower, and Heinrich Stahl.

That the "self-administration" in Theresienstadt was merely an instrument of the ss camp guard and had absolutely nothing to do with democratic functions and self-determination requires no further elaboration. However, this needs to be emphasized to counter the myth that there was indeed room for maneuver that was not fully utilized. If the self-administration in the ghetto at Theresienstadt is described as the remains of the Reichsvereinigung, then the level of cultural life has to be understood in the same way: the reports of theater performances, operas, recitals, and academic lectures, so predominant in memoirs, the last activities of the brave artists and organizers of the Jüdischer Kulturbund (Association for Jewish Culture), continuing in Theresienstadt what they had begun in Germany—all these activities should not lead to the false conclusion that Theresienstadt was an oasis of

German-Jewish culture, a kind of summer academy in which Goethe was recited and Mozart played from dawn to dusk.

The inmates of Theresienstadt perceived the self-administration as the top of the camp hierarchy that meted out punishment, passed laws, and conducted a monstrous bureaucracy. The nasty phrase was coined, "Strafhaft in Theresienstadt, verschärft durch jüdische Selbstverwaltung" (penal service in Theresienstadt, made worse by the Jewish self-administration). However, on reflection, some people felt relief that the inmates were not required to have any direct contact with the ss.

Viewed from below, the "Jewish elder" appeared to be the absolute master of the ghetto. He was in regular contact with the ss command to whom he reported and from whom he received orders. Recruited from Berlin by the National Socialists for this purpose, Dr. Paul Eppstein occupied the position of "Jewish elder" from January 1943 until September 1944. A man in his early forties, he was soon extremely unpopular, a fact for which he himself was only partially responsible. On January 27, 1943, camp commander and ss captain Dr. Seidl had sent for the incumbent Jewish elder Jacob Edelstein, a native of Prague. On behalf of Adolf Eichmann he informed him that important officials from Berlin and Vienna were expected on the following day. Therefore the responsibilities in Theresienstadt had to be rearranged. From now on Dr. Eppstein from Berlin would bear the main responsibility for the self-administration of the ghetto and would head a triumvirate that would also include Edelstein.

Eppstein got off to a poor start and did not enjoy good press in Theresienstadt. For posterity, the character and deeds of Dr. Eppstein have been documented in H. G. Adler's monumental account of the *Zwangsgemeinschaft* (enforced community) in Theresienstadt. Adler's appraisal is as unequivocal as is it devastating, even if one chooses to ignore his moral judgments:

Although Eppstein was ambitious, he lacked courage. . . . He was a poseur, theatrical, soft and vain. . . . One had the impression that he presented the Jewish cause to the ss meekly and without resistance; he took the orders and carried them out. Certainly Eppstein was not devoid of humanity, given his depressed personality, but he was not known for his warmth and kindness. . . . Eppstein referred to himself as a socialist Zionist; at the same time, he admired power, even as represented by the National Socialists. . . . Inside the camp he was seen only as a weak man, always trying to escape from the present that terrified him and whose corrupting character had already left him a hollow shell.

Adler's characterization of Eppstein has not met with universal approval. Coworkers of Eppstein have spoken out and demanded a fairer assessment. Jacob Jacobson pointed out that the leaders of the central Jewish organizations had found themselves in the terrible predicament "of being forced to act as loyal minions of the authorities and even assist in the preparations for the deportations." Similarly, the Jewish elders and their subordinates in Theresienstadt were forced to prepare the death transports to the East "as ordered." Is it fair to condemn them for this? Every "Jewish elder" and every member of his council was aware of the fact that the work of deception and destruction was in keeping with the instructions of the government. They had no choice but to comply while at the same time attempting to ease the lot of their fellow inmates as much as possible. Nobody, regardless of their strength of character, could have deflected the attacks of the Nazi regime under these circumstances. Who can pass judgment on someone who occupied a position of authority and tried to delay these assaults?

According to Jacobson's plea, if Eppstein was not without human weaknesses, it does nothing to alter the fact that even through actions open to criticism he merely tried to do the best for his charges, namely, to improve their lot and to save as many as possible from physical destruction. At the same time, his failure to succeed led to his downfall. As proof of this Jacobson documented the following:

One day before Rosh Hashanah in 1944 he gave an almost suicidal speech in front of more than a thousand prisoners. At that time the appearance of American planes over Theresienstadt provoked an understandable outburst of rejoicing, and Eppstein warned against premature hopes and actions. On Yom Kippur 1944 he was arrested and shot on the same day. It was generally believed among the inmates that Eppstein was killed because of his protests against the mass deportations that had commenced at the time.

Eppstein's biography, in addition to providing clues to the understanding of his role in Theresienstadt, probably offers some insights into the state of mind and the emotions of German Jewry at the time of their destruction. Paul Eppstein was born on March 4, 1901, in Mannheim. Noted as a highly gifted pupil, he went on to study philosophy, economics, and sociology in Heidelberg and Freiburg. Having studied under Max Weber, Karl Mannheim, Karl Jaspers, and Alfred Weber, he qualified as a lecturer at the age of twenty-five at the Handelshochschule (College of Commerce) in Mannheim, a position he held until 1933. The destruction of his academic career must surely have had a traumatic effect on the young Paul Eppstein. As a convicted Zionist he was actively involved in the Jewish youth movement. He played a leading role in the Reichsausschuss der jüdischen Jugendverbände (Reich Council of Jewish Youth Associations), which earned him posts in the Zentralwohlfahrtsstelle der deutschen Juden e.V. (Central Welfare Bureau of German Jews) and, from 1933 on, a full-time position in the Reichsvereinigung der Juden in Deutschland. There Eppstein was responsible first for loans, then for emigration. In this role he functioned as a liaison officer with the Gestapo. In all likelihood he was isolated even further by a four-month incarceration in the police prison at Alexanderplatz, which he was forced to endure for allegedly sabotaging illegal migration to Palestine. Indeed, the reason for his imprisonment provides a key to his personality: he had refused to comply with the Gestapo, who, without consideration for the British restrictions and hence the fate of the defrauded Jewish migrants to Palestine, was only interested at the time in getting the Jews out of the country. Eppstein apparently had pressed for an orderly process and thus raised the ire of the Gestapo.

In Theresienstadt order and correctness are thus key principles for the Jewish elder Eppstein, which he vigorously implemented, to the incomprehension of many. The value of propagating the work ethic and punctuality within the misery of Theresienstadt was met with skepticism by many who viewed the Jewish elder, with his bureaucratic and executive apparatus, which extended from messenger boy to ghetto guard, as only the embodiment of German values that they themselves had honored until their banishment. The upholding of middle-class intellectual achievements in discussion groups, with lectures, theater performances, and concerts went without saying for the Theresienstadt community. It was indeed expected of Paul Eppstein that he conduct regular seminars in sociology. However, his propagation and implemetation of orderliness as well as his playing the part of "mayor" during the visits of delegations struck many as incredible.

Eppstein's tragedy lay in the simple fact that, in whatever he undertook, he had only the methods of a middle-class academic at his disposal. He had had no other training. It was his dilemma that his existence in Theresienstadt was by definition two-faced: he could be an aid to the Jews only by attempting to gain the confidence of their torturers. He shared this situation with others. Even those critical of this attitude, which by necessity was the one adopted by other Jewish functionaries, concede that alternatives such as vehement resistance did not exist.

Eppstein's fate, as the Jewish elder of Theresienstadt who was repeatedly betrayed by the Nazis, who was stripped of all his privileges and shot on September 27, 1944, and whose wife was deported from Theresienstadt with the last transport to Auschwitz and murdered there, is more than a personal tragedy. He found himself in the typical situation of those German Jews who, for whatever personal reasons, had accepted responsibilities from the National Socialists, and, in the search for justice, these prominent individuals should be judged solely within this context.

Following an order issued by the Nazis a propaganda film was made in Theresienstadt in August and September 1944 that later became known by the ironic title *Der Führer schenkt den Juden eine Stadt* (The Führer gives the Jews a city). The actual working title of the film, which remained a fragment and was never shown in cinemas, was "Theresienstadt.

Ein Dokumentarfilm aus dem jüdischen Siedlungsgebiet"
(Theresienstadt: A Documentary from the Jewish Settlement). In June 1943 the National Socialists permitted a del-
egation from the Red Cross to visit camps that had been
especially prepared for them as well as for the filming.

The visit to Theresiensatdt remained, of course, without
any real consequences. Yet, despite the staged pseudo-real-
ity of a pleasant life in the camp, the visitors were obviously
left with some impressions that were closer to reality, as is
made clear by the notes of an official from the International Red Cross:

The gentlemen from the Red Cross spent forty-eight hours in
Theresienstadt and were left with strong impressions of the
camp, i.e., they were filled with deep consternation. It was in
fact the first time that representatives of the Red Cross had had
any direct contact with deportees. In Theresienstadt itself there
were 43,800 Jews. Of these, two-thirds had work of some kind,
one-third were unfit to work at all. The average age of the
inmates was 60. The situation in the ghetto was horrific. There
was not enough of anything. The people were shockingly
undernourished and medical assistance was totally unsatisfactory. The living conditions were horrific—in a town that had
once sustained 7,000 people there were now between six and
seven times as many. In one building, where a group of so-
called prominent inmates were housed (including a member of
the Bleichroeder family), there were four to five people living
in one room. In the living quarters of the ordinary people the

situation was much worse. At least the organization of the ghetto was such that everything that could be done was being done. There were public kitchens, kindergartens, hospitals. In the town itself there were several shops where a number of things could be purchased. Within the ghetto a special form of legal tender was in circulation, which was covered by money kept in accounts at certain banks (probably a part of the sequestered Jewish assets).

Part of the reality of Theresienstadt were flunctuations in its population. If the journey to Theresienstadt was undertaken unwillingly, so too was the departure from the ghetto. The population peaked in September 1942 at 53,004. In that month 18,639 arrived at the ghetto while 13,004 were deported from it to an extermination camp. During that month alone 3,941 died in Theresienstadt. During the first half of 1943 there was a decline in the number of new arrivals, but the deportations continued. Until September 1942 the final destinations after Theresienstadt included Riga, Treblinka, Minsk, Sobibor, Majdanek, Izbica, and Zamosc. From October 1942 on, the trains were headed for only one destination: Auschwitz. After the last wave of deportations in Autumn 1944, there were only 11,068 Jews remaining in Theresienstadt, among them 456 Danish and 4,843 Dutch Jews.

At the end of April 1945 evacuation transports with prisoners from a number of concentration camps arrived in Theresienstadt. They numbered approximately 14,000.

On May 5, 1945, the responsibility for Theresienstadt was handed over by the National Socialists to the Red Cross; on May 8 the Red Army arrived. Theresienstadt was in fact the last camp to be liberated. The high mortality rate persisted after liberation—the poor health of many inmates prevented them from leaving the ghetto. The last to leave could not do so until August 17, 1945.

The total figures for Theresienstadt were as follows: between November 24, 1941, and April 20, 1945, 141,000 Jews were deported there, 33,000 died there, and 88,000 were deported on from there to an extermination camp.

Two of the three commandants, Dr. Siegfried Seidl (December 1941 to June 1943) and Karl Rahm (February 1944 to May 1945) were sentenced to death after the war and executed. The third, ss-Obersturmführer Anton Burger (commandant from July 1943 until February 1944), established a new existence for himself under a false name in postwar Germany. Despite all the efforts to track him down, he was not discovered and died in Essen at the end of 1991.

11. THE OTHER GENOCIDE:
The Persecution of the Sinti and Roma

As elsewhere in Europe, there existed in Germany a tradition of discrimination against the "Gypsies." Long before

1933 mistrust and rejection of the Sinti and Roma minority found their expression in a plethora of laws and decrees of exclusion. Feelings of contempt and rejection, even the desire to see the "Gypsies" eradicated, were expressed more widely and openly than those toward the Jewish minority, however unwelcome they too were "on racial grounds." The National Socialist policy toward the "Gypsies" led as unswervingly toward genocide as did the policy toward the Jews, and for that reason the persecution of the Roma and Sinti must be viewed within the framework of the Holocaust.

Long before the National Socialists came to power, the authorities at local, city, and state levels in Germany as well as Austria were officially in agreement that the best way to deal with the "Gypsy plague" was to educate the "Gypsies" in a settled form of existence and so integrate them into German society. This intention was publicly declared again and again. The citizens, however, were also in agreement that the settlement of the "Gypsies" always should take place somewhere else, never in their own community. Harassment of the Roma and Sinti in Germany after 1933 continued at first in the usual way—inflated rental costs and poorly equipped campsites (and apartments), police raids, sudden closure of campsites and expulsion from municipal areas, restrictions in the issuing of permits mandatory for itinerant trading—the very basis of this people's economic existence. Under the influence of the NSDAP there was a gradual development toward ghettoization. Many large cities set up campsites, which were in part guarded and fenced in with barbed wire and always poorly situated, often in taboo locations such as close to cemeteries or sewage plants.

This was followed by a deterioration of the legal position of the Roma and Sinti through the centralization of the police and the rapid implementation of new racial policies in the now established Nazi regime. Although "Gypsies" were not specifically mentioned, the Nuremberg Laws also applied to this minority and turned them formally into second-class citizens. In 1938 a Reichszentrale zur Bekämpfung des Zigeunerunwesens (Reich Central Office to Combat the Gypsy Menace) was established within the Reich Criminal Police Office. Heinrich Himmler, under whose jurisdiction as "Reichsführer ss and chief of the German Police" the Sinti and Roma fell, decreed on December 8, 1938, that "any settlement of the Gypsy question must result from the very nature of this race" and should be based on "knowledge stemming from ethnological research." Researchers with the Criminal Police, who worked under Dr. Robert Ritter at the Rassenhygienischen Forschungsstelle (Research Institute for Racial Hygiene) within the Reich Health Department, were to provide the necessary documentation.

The experts approached their task with complete thoroughness and produced for the Criminal Police detailed reports based on geneological and anthropological studies. In the final analysis the subjects of the research were divided into distinct categories, into "Gypsies" of mixed blood (who were then subdivided into the categories of "predominantly Gypsy blood" and "predominantly German blood"). This preoccupation with "racial hygiene" served the practical purpose of separating out those deemed undesirable and inferior for extermination.

The police and their expert helpers had in no way acted on their own in declaring a war of destruction on the Roma and Sinti minority. The extermination of the "Gypsies" was an integral part of the stated aims of Nazi racial politics. One of the many pieces of evidence for this is the letter sent by Reich justice minister Thierack to the chief of the Party Chancellery of the NSDAP, Martin Bormann, in June 1942:

Guided by the idea of freeing the German national organism of Poles, Russians, Jews, and Gypsies, as well as by the idea of clearing the eastern districts annexed to the Reich, which are earmarked for the settlement of German nationals, I intend to hand over the criminal prosecution of Poles, Russians, Jews, and Gypsies to the Reichsführer ss. In doing so I am assuming that the penal system can make only a limited contribution to the extermination of these ethnic groups. This is not due to any doubts that the law will pass very harsh judgment indeed against these people, but that it will not suffice to see in principle the ideas expressed above realized. There is little sense in keeping these people locked up for years in German prisons and other penal institutions, not even if, as is often the case today, they are put to work in the war effort.

This letter had been preceded by a conference on September 18, 1942, at which Himmler discussed the future direction of punishment of "foreign peoples" with high-ranking ss officials. In Himmler's view—and together with the police and ss he possessed the instruments of terror for pursuing the extreme aims of the regime—the fate of some groups of people no longer fell within the jurisdiction of the law and the courts: "Asocial elements sentenced to prison terms are to be handed over to the Reichsführer ss to be worked to death. All Jews, Gypsies, Russians, Ukrainians, and Poles, arrested for security reasons and given sentences of more than three years, should be handed over." There were practical considerations why the officials directly affected, the Gauleiter of the NSDAP in the annexed eastern districts as well as the Reich minister for the interior and the Reich minister for the East, protested against taking such measures against Poles and Russians. It could undermine the willingness to work and the recruitment of Polish, Russian, and Ukrainian foreign workers and could possibly be seized upon by the enemy propoganda machine. The "doing away with the criminal prosecution of Jews and 'Gypsies,'" however, was deemed correct and desirable by these same officials. In reality, this meant that the Sinti and Roma were stripped of all rights and, as such, were at the mercy of the police and ss.

Long before Himmler's decree, however, in which the racially motivated "war against the Gypsy plague" was declared, the Sinti amd Roma were persecuted and, from the spring of 1938 on, placed in "protective custody" within concentration camps. The pretext used was the traditional accusation that the "Gypsies" were "asocial," proof of which lay in their inability to engage in "regular work." Schutzhaft, that is, the loss of freedom in a concentration camp, without a trial and for an unspecified period of time, was the weapon most widely used in the Nazi state against minorities, critics, and opponents of the regime. From an early stage, however, many made a case that more drastic measures be taken against the Sinti and Roma.

In 1939 an Austrian National Socialist, the provincial governor of Burgenland, wrote to the chief of the Reich Chancellery, Reich Minister Lammers:

For reasons that are in the interest of the health of the people, and because it has been proven that certain unfavorable qualities are hereditary among the Gypsies and that they are a people of perennial criminals who live as parasites among our population and cause monstrous damage, our first task should be to prevent them from breeding further and to subject those now alive to a strict work routine within the framework of a labor camp.

In time, that demand for sterilization was to be articulated with increasing regularity and, indeed, was finally put into practice. The "intense breeding of the Gypsies" was constantly used as an argument, and its logical conclusion appeared to be rendering the undesired ethnic group sterile. This is also made clear in a letter of 1940 by the public prosecutor of Graz in which he clearly proposes the sterilization of all the Roma in Burgenland:

The Gypsies live almost exclusively from begging and stealing. Working as musicians is more of a smokescreen than an actual form of employment. Their presence is an extraordinarily heavy burden on the remaining population of honest workers, especially on the farmers whose fields they plunder, a burden that is growing year by year due to a breeding rate that remains extraordinarily high despite an also high infant mortality rate. The danger for the racial purity of the Burgenland population is even greater. The great mass of the Gypsies, who by their external appearance alone remind one rather more of African or Asian primitive peoples, are racially inferior, especially intellectually and morally, yet at the same time they are physically extraordinarily resilient, as the children who survive from the great number of infants born grow up under extremely harsh living conditions. Any interbreeding with this morally and intellectually inferior people inevitably means a decline in the values of the offspring. Interbreeding, however, is aided, on the one hand, by the fact that young male Gypsies are sexually extremely aggressive, on the other hand, by the promiscuity of the Gypsy girls. These circumstances are not altered if the majority of male Gypsies are accommodated in labor camps.

Such stereotypes, particularly those jealously alluding to sexual aggressiveness and promiscuity, corresponded to widespread images of "Gypsies" within the general population. So it was then that calls for racially motivated harsh treatment found considerable resonance and were met with large-scale actions that went unopposed, similar to the policies adopted against the Jews.

For the National Socialist regime the Second World War served as a welcome backdrop for the planned annihilation of undesirable minorities that, if necessary, could also be used in public as a justification for their measures. On September 2, 1939, the "moving around of Gypsies and other persons wandering in Gypsy style" was outlawed in the border districts of the German Reich. This could be explained away with little difficulty as a war measure, and on October 17, 1939, the RSHA issued an order that "Gypsies and half-Gypsies" were no longer permitted to leave their permanent or transient place of residence.

This Festschreibungserlass (decree restricting freedom of movement) signaled the final stage of persecution. It became the duty of the local police to keep count of the Sinti and Roma (hence the order for a settled form of existence) and to classify them according to categories set out in racial policy and the "preventive war against crime." At the end of September 1939 the decision had been made to first deport the suspected "thirty thousand Gypsies" living on German soil to Poland, a fate they shared with the Jews. The expulsion of the undesirables to a newly conquered and submissive Poland represented, in fact, the first step on the road to their annihilation. In the eastern territories, which were ruled and treated like colonies, the planned mass murder could be better camouflaged and consideration of the civilian population hardly appeared necessary.

On May 16, 1940, the organized deportation of the Roma and Sinti in families from the length and breadth of the German Reich began. On April 27 Himmler had ordered the Criminal Police Headquarters in Hamburg, Bremen, Cologne, Düsseldorf, Hanover, Frankfurt/Main, and Stuttgart to arrest the Sinti and Roma living in their districts and intern them in transit camps. From there they were herded together into transports whose destination was occupied Poland. This action, which claimed the lives of approximately twenty-eight hundred human beings—a tenth of all Sinti and Roma living in Germany—represented a type of dress rehearsal for genocide. The RSHA in Berlin issued quotas: one thousand from each of the districts of Hamburg and Bremen, Cologne, Düsseldorf and Hanover, five hundred from Frankfurt and Stuttgart. Selection of the individual families was left up to the local Criminal Police. They based their selection on the "racial reports" of the experts at the Reich Health Department, who were on hand to assist in the selection of the deportees. The families were transported from three transit camps (Hohenasperg, near Stuttgart, Cologne, and Hamburg) by special trains to Poland and in various camps there subjected to the torments of the harshest forced labor—children and old people, sick and healthy alike were forced to work up to fourteen hours daily.

On December 16, 1942, Heinrich Himmler, master of concentration and extermination camps, issued an order that paved the way for the final episode in the murderous chapter of discrimination and persecution against the Sinti and Roma. The RSHA drew up the guidelines for its implementation. On January 29, 1943, it was decreed:

By order of the Reichsführer SS on December 16, 1942. . . . Gypsies of mixed blood, Rom-Gypsies, and members of Gypsy clans of Balkan origin who have no German blood are to be selected according to specific guidelines and sent to concentration camps in an operation lasting only a few weeks. This group of people is hereafter to be referred to as "Gypsy-like persons." There is to be no consideration of the degree of mixed blood and deportation should be in family groups to the concentration camp at Auschwitz. The Gypsy question will be settled through a special decree in the "Gaue" of the Alps and Danube River. The future treatment of the racially pure Sinti Gypsies and the Lalleri Gypsies and their clans classified as racially pure will be determined by a later regulation.

The victims were arrested in secrecy in family groups. They were forced to leave all their possessions behind; identification papers, money, and valuables were taken—in other words, stolen from them. Via prisons and various transit camps these people finally reached Auschwitz-

Birkenau, where they were housed in a separate area of the extermination camp and forced to live in deplorable conditions. In witness accounts one can read: "When it rained, everything was drenched and the prisoners were up to their knees in mud. The Gypsies realized straight after their arrival what was going on. After all, the crematoria were close by. So they hid their infants under their skirts or wrapped them in blankets."

Once again the prisoners were at the mercy of *Forscher* (experts) in racial politics, including the notorious camp doctor Mengele, who subjected many of them to pseudoscientific experiments. One night at the beginning of August 1943 the entire "Gypsy camp" of Auschwitz was liquidated. One eyewitness reported on the liquidation during the Auschwitz trial held in Frankfurt in 1964:

There were terrible scenes. Women and children were kneeling in front of Mengele and Boger and calling out: "Mercy! Have mercy!" It was all to no avail. They were brutally beaten and kicked and pushed onto the lorries. It was a terrible, cruel night. . . . Those who had been beaten lay motionless on the ground and were tossed onto the lorries.

In the course of the Holocaust the genocide of the Sinti and Roma was carried out in many places within the National Socialist sphere of power—in the extermination camps of Auschwitz, Chelmno/Kulmhof, Treblinka, and Majdanek on Polish soil, through mass executions in

Poland and in the Baltic states, in Croatia and Serbia, in Ukraine, on the Crimean peninsula. Apart from the ss and police, Gestapo and military police, the perpetrators included Latvian and Ukrainian militia, Croatian Ustashi-fascists, Slovakian Hlinka guardsmen, Serbs, and many others who assisted the Germans in the implementation of their racial policies.

The number of victims is more difficult to determine in this case than in that of the Jews. Because of their lifestyle the Roma living in Eastern and Southern Europe were largely excluded from statistical records. Documentary evidence of the mass murder is imprecise and scant, both because in many cases it did not exist and because for a long time nobody made the effort to locate it. There can be no doubt that more than two hundred thousand Sinti and Roma fell victim to the National Socialist genocide. Some estimates are as high as half a million. As was not the case with the Jews, they had to wait a long time after their persecution before they found help or even understanding. In respect to the claims of the Sinti and Roma for compensation for the persecution they suffered, the German compensation authorities, in full agreement with politicians and public opinion, argued well into the 1970s that the "Gypsies" were in fact sent to the concentration camps by and large as criminals and asocials and as such became victims of state measures. In other words, they and they alone were to blame for any persecution they endured. It was only fitting, then, that personal files and other documents relating to the minority of Sinti and Roma from the Nazi period should be used. It took a civil rights movement initiated by the Sinti and Roma themselves to arouse sympathy among the German population not only for current discrimination but also for persecution suffered in the past.

12. INDUSTRIALIZED MASS MURDER IN THE EXTERMINATION CAMPS, 1942–1944

Auschwitz is a place in Poland not far from Krakow, situated between the rivers Sola and Weichsel at the Moravian Gap between the Sudeten and Carpathian mountain ranges, on the former border of the German Reich. Before World War I the town was part of the Austro-Hungarian Empire. In 1939, after the brutal occupation of Poland, Oswiecim was incorporated into the German Reich and renamed Auschwitz once again. In spring 1940 the Reichsführer ss and chief of the German police Himmler ordered that a camp be set up there. Former Polish artillery barracks, in which the Austrian military were garrisoned in the nineteenth century, formed the nucleus of the main camp Auschwitz onward from May 20, 1940. It was originally intended as a transit camp, but during the four and a half years that it was operational Auschwitz developed into the largest exploitation and extermination complex within the National Socialist imperium. In Auschwitz prisoners from the concentration camp were recruited as slave labor for German industry. Auschwitz was the greatest machine of murder that had ever been conceived and then realized. Auschwitz lay beyond the powers of the human imagination.

Some kilometers away in Auschwitz-Monowitz, camp 3, and in thirty-eight satellite camps, prisoners were forced to work for German industry until they had not an ounce of strength left in them. Auschwitz-Birkenau, camp 2, accessible by rail, with a selection ramp, was established at the end of November 1941, three kilometers northwest of the main camp, and became the real factory of death. This is where the transports of Jews from throughout Europe arrived; this is where, immediately following their arrival, those deemed fit to work were separated by the ss from those sent immediately to the gas chambers, without any further bureaucratic procedures such as registration, prisoner numbers, or tatooing. It was in Birkenau that Dr. Josef Mengele and other perverted doctors carried out their medical "experiments," and it was here that Sinti and Roma vegetated in the "Gypsy camp" until their murder one August night in 1944.

The nucleus of the complex was the main camp, which first served as the concentration camp for Poland, then became the site of the first gas chamber in which the mass extermination of human life was tried and tested. The camp commandant was (until November 1943) Rudolf Hess, previously an ss–Obersturmbannführer (as such, equal in rank with Adolf Eichmann), who built up and ran the factory of death with the organizational talents of a manager and reported about it afterward with the meticulousness of a bookkeeper. Rudolf Hess, born in 1900, had been active as a right-wing extremist until he joined the ss in 1934, did service in the concentration camps at Dachau and Sachsenhausen, and, following his time in Auschwitz, climbed the career ladder until being made deputy section head in the ss Economic and Administration Main Office, the highest administrative authority for all the concentration camps. In March 1946 he was arrested by the British military police, was witness at the Nuremberg trials, and appeared then in Kraków before his judges, who sentenced him to death on April 2, 1947. He was executed two weeks later at Auschwitz, the very place where he had been active himself.

Hess reported in detail about his role in the mass murder and before his death completed some autobigraphical writings. In the summer of 1941 Hess had been ordered to Berlin and learned there from Himmler that Auschwitz was to be afforded a key role in the Final Solution of the Jewish question. The Reichsführer ss explained to Hess:

It is tough and difficult work, which requires the commitment of your entire self, without consideration of difficulties that may arise in the course of it. You will be given more details by

Sturmbannführer Eichmann from the RSHA, who will come to see you in the near future. The offices involved will be informed by me in due time. You are to maintain absolute silence about this order, even toward your superiors. After the meeting with Eichmann, immediately send me the plans of the proposed site. The Jews are the eternal enemies of the German people and must be eradicated. All Jews accessible to us are, without exception, to be annihilated now in the course of the war. If we do not succeed now in destroying the foundations of Jewry, the time will come when the Jews will annihilate the German people. . . . A short time after that, Eichmann came to see me at Auschwitz. He instructed me about the plans for the actions in the various countries. I can no longer recall the exact order.

At first East Upper Silesia and the bordering districts of the General Government were the areas of relevance for Auschwitz—at the same time, and in a type of geographical progression, the Jews from Germany and Czechoslovakia. Next the west: France, Belgium, Holland. He gave me the approximate numbers of the transports that we could expect. . . . We spoke further about the implementation of the extermination. It seemed that only gas came into question, because disposing of the masses that you could expect from shooting would be virtually impossible and also too great a burden for the ss men who would have to carry it out, also in the case of women and children. Eichmann familiarized me with killing by exhaust fumes in trucks, as had already been practiced in the East. However, in the case of the mass transports that were expected in Auschwitz, this would be out of the question. Killing by carbon monoxide, through showers in a bathroom, as was implemented to exterminate the mentally disturbed at some locations in the Reich, required too many buildings, and obtaining the gas for the great masses would be very problematic. We came to no decision on this matter. Eichmann wanted to inquire after a gas that would be easy to obtain and require no special facilities and then report back to me. We drove into the countryside to choose a suitable spot. We thought the farmstead at the northwestern corner of what later became construction stage 3, Birkenau, would be suitable. It was remote enough, shielded from view by surrounding woods and hedges, and not too far from the train line.

On September 3, 1941, in the cellar of block 11 in the main camp, the use of the disinfestation material cyclon B was first trialed in the killing of human beings. Himmler had issued instructions that a method be found to implement the "Final Solution of the Jewish question" as rationally and effectively as possible. In place of the pogroms and massacres, the shootings and beatings, there was now to be perfectly organized mass murder, which was to run without a hitch. After the first trial Hess had one room of the crematorium in the main camp set up as a gas chamber. The doors of the original mortuary (which was 16.8 m long and 4.6 m wide) were insulated, vents built into the roof through which the gas would be released (the gas was combined with silicic acid, in a quasi-crystalline form, and delivered in cans by the firms Tesch and Stabenow in Hamburg and Degesch in Frankfurt/Main), and a ventilation system installed. In this gas chamber ninety-nine Russian prisoners of war were the first to be killed. The operation met with the full satisfaction of the murderers.

In Birkenau (Auschwitz II) one of the farm houses that Hess and Eichmann inspected was converted into a gas chamber; at the end of June a second one was converted as well. They became known as Bunker 1 and Bunker 2. At the end of 1942 Bunker 1 was demolished and replaced by a large crematorium (with two gas chambers). The transports of victims to Auschwitz began in spring 1942—first the Jews from Upper Silesia and then from all corners of occupied Europe. The transports reached their height in summer 1944 with the deportation of the Jews from Hungary; a late tragedy was the transport of eighteen hundred Greek Jews from the island of Rhodes to Auschwitz at the end of July 1944. To cope with the murders, the capacity of the extermination camp was increased through several new stages of construction. At the end there were four crematoria in operation for burning the bodies. The gas chambers, which were camouflaged as shower rooms, included barracks where the victims were forced to get undressed. In another complex clothes and valuables, suitcases, spectacles, and hair were sorted into piles for reuse.

As the transports arrived, up to 90 percent of the deportees were selected as unfit to work and herded into the gas chambers. The same fate was planned for those whose remaining strength was to be exploited for work, as soon they were totally exhausted.

Max Mannheimer, born in 1920 in Neutitschein in Czechoslovakia, was a graduate of a commercial college and had completed a business apprenticeship. He was deported to Auschwitz in January 1943 after he had passed through the stations that were usual for Jews from Bohemia and Moravia—forced labor and then Theresienstadt. On the same transport were his parents, his young wife, his sister, his sister-in-law, and two brothers:

Auschwitz-Birkenau, death ramp, midnight on February 1, 1943. Everyone out! Leave everything behind! Panic. Everyone tries to stuff as much as possible into their pockets. The ss people are screaming: Come on! Get a move on! Another shirt is put on. Another pullover. Cigarettes. Perhaps as a bargaining object. Men on this side, women on the other side, women with children onto the trucks. Men and women who have trouble walking can go by truck. Many put up their hand. The rest are placed into rows of five. One women tries to come over to us. Presumably she wants to speak to her husband or son. An ss man pulls her to the ground with a walking stick. By the neck. She doesn't move. Is dragged away. To a work detail?

An ss officer is standing in front of us. Obersturmführer. Addressed by a guard. Probably a doctor. Without a white coat. Without a stethoscope. In a green uniform. With the death's head insignia. One by one we step forward. His voice is calm. Almost too calm. He asks our age, profession, whether we are healthy. Has himself shown hands. I hear some of the answers.

137

Locksmith—left. Administrator—right. Doctor—left. Laborer
—left. Storeman with the firm Bata—right. It's an acquaintance
of ours. Büchler from Bojkowitz. Carpenter—left. Then it's my
father's turn. Unskilled worker. He goes the same way as the
administrator and the storeman. He is fifty-five. That could be
the reason. Now me. Twenty-three years old, healthy, road
construction worker. Calluses on my hands. How good the calluses are. Left. My brother Ernst: twenty, plumber—left. My
brother Edgar: seventeen, shoemaker—left. Try to locate my
mother, wife, sister, sister-in-law. It's impossible. Many trucks
have left.

Placed in rows of three. An ss guard asks for Czech cigarettes. I give him some. He answers my questions. The children
attend kindergarten. Men can visit their wives on Sundays.
Only on Sundays? That's not enough! It will have to be enough.

We march. On a narrow road. We can see a brightly lit
square. In the middle of the war. No black out. Watch towers
with MGs. Two barbed wire fences, searchlights, barracks. ss
guards open a gate. We march through. We are in Birkenau.
We stop for ten minutes in front of some barracks. Then we are
allowed in. There are now 155 men from the transport from the
1,000 men, women, and children. Several prisoners are sitting at
tables. Money and valuables are to be handed over. Also anything hidden. Otherwise there are harsh penalties. I undo a
piece of my shirt collar. Ten-dollar notes. From my father-in-
law. As a reserve for hard times. The names are registered. I ask
whether I should keep my identity card. No, is the answer. We
would get new ones. We go outside. Then more barracks. In

one room we take off our clothes. We keep only shoes and belts. All our hair is cut off. And shaved off. On account of the lice. We are sprayed with cuprex (a lice disinfectant). Enter a very warm room. Built in the form of steps. Like a sauna. We are naked and enjoy the warmth. We look strange. Odd. Bald, belts around our bare stomachs, and we have shoes on. A prisoner in striped clothing comes in. He stands in front of us. We ask after the women, children. "Go through the furnace!" We don't understand him. We think he's a sadist. We don't ask any more questions.

From the end of October 1944 the extermination facilities in Auschwitz-Birkenau were destroyed on orders from Himmler so as to leave no traces for the Red Army (which will free Auschwitz at the end of January 1945). The crematoria together with the gas chambers were blown up. The exact number of victims of the murder machine at Auschwitz is not known. Before the Nuremberg tribunal Hess gave a figure of 2.5 million, which is too high and is used by right-wing extremists who deny the Holocaust as proof that all claims about Auschwitz are false and that nothing in fact was the way survivors testify that it was, which is confirmed by perpetrators. The number of murders commited in Auschwitz between January 1942 and November 1944, the period in which the gas chambers were fully operational, is about 1 million. As such, the camp at Auschwitz was the largest extermination site of the Holocaust.

Only one other camp can be seen as comparable with Auschwitz, where the extermination site arose out of the concentration camp and the dual functions of exploitation and extermination were pursued concurrently. This camp was set up in autumn 1941 in the district capital city of Lublin. Its extermination site became known by the name of Majdanek (a district in Lublin). Before its liberation in July 1944 by Soviet and Polish troops and during the entire time it was in existence approximately two hundred thousand people lost their lives in Majdanek, among them around sixty thousand Jews. The phase of the extermination operations lasted from summer 1942 until July 1944. As in Auschwitz, cyclon B was used in the murders in addition to carbon monoxide, which was delivered to the camp in steel flasks and fed through pipes into the gas chambers. In autumn 1943 there were once again, as in the time of the Einsatzgruppen, massacres in which the victims were murdered in shooting operations.

On November 3, 1943, the carefully prepared operation took place that became known by the prisoners as "Bloody Wednesday" and "Operation Harvest Festival" by the perpetrators. On that one day all Jews from the concentration camp who had been working in the ss-run "German armaments works" and in work details outside the camp fell victim to this operation. It claimed almost eighteen thousand lives. The chief of the crematorium, Erich Muhsfeldt, gave an eyewitness report:

One day at the end of October, behind fields V and VI, about
50 m from the new crematorium, pits were dug out. Around
300 prisoners carried out the work in day and night shifts of 150
men each for three days. In the course of these three days three
zigzag pits measuring over 2 m deep and approximately 100 m
long were dug out. At the same time, Sonderkommandos (special commandos) from the concentration camp at Auschwitz
and the ss and police headquarters in Kraków, Warsaw, Radom,
Lemberg, and Lublin arrived in Majdanek. All together about
100 ss people from all the places I have mentioned came and
formed the Sonderkommandos.

The watchtowers around the camp received reinforce-
ments during the night and at morning roll call on
November 3 all the Jews were singled out. Jewish prisoners from the satellite camps and Aussenkommandos
marched in a long file.

At about 6 o'clock in the morning—perhaps it was already
about 7 o'clock—the operation began. Some of the Jews on
field V were herded into barracks where they all had to get
completely undressed. Then Thumann, the commander of the
protective custody section, cut through the barbed wire
between field V and the pit. A passageway appeared on this
meadow. From there as far as the pit armed police formed a cordon. Through this cordon the naked Jews were hustled toward
the pits. There they were ordered by an ss man from the Sonderkommando to climb into the pit in groups of ten. Those

who were already in the pit were pushed to one end. There they were forced to lie down. Then they were shot by the ss people from the Sonderkommando standing at the edge of the pit. Then it was the turn of the next groups to be pushed to the end of the pit. There they had to lie down on top of those who had already been shot, so that in time the pit was filled section by section almost to the top. Men and women were shot in separate groups. The operation went on without interruption until 5 o'clock in the afternoon. The ss people who had taken part in the shootings were relieved. They drove to the ss barracks in the city for a meal, while the operation continued without a break. The whole time it was going on music was playing through the loudspeakers.

At the Wannsee Conference the representative of the General Government, State Secretary Bühler, had requested that the "Jewish Question" be solved as quickly as possible in his district. That was in January 1942. Included in his arguments were the claims that most of the estimated 2.5 million Jews in the General Government were unfit to work anyway, that as disease carriers they represented an imminent danger, and that fortunately there were no particular transport hurdles in the way of annihilation.

The preparations for the eradication of the Jews in occupied Poland, in the districts within the General Government of Warsaw, KraKów, Lublin, Radom, and Lemberg, were in fact well underway at that time. The man responsible for them was ss Brigadeführer Odilo Globocnik, an Austrian born in Triest who had joined the NSDAP in 1922 in Kärnten and subsequently joined the ss in 1932. In 1938–1939 he had been gauleiter of Vienna, until he was dismissed from this post for misappropriating funds. In November 1939 the thirty-five year old received his second career opening as ss and police chief of the district of Lublin. As the man responsible for the implementation of the order to annihilate the Jews of Poland, Globocnik was directly answerable to Reichsführer ss Himmler (in accordance to rank and the official channels of command, however, he remained subordinate to the higher ss and police chief of the General Government, ss Obergruppenführer Friedrich Krüger).

The staff attached to "Operation Reinhard"—the name was given by the undersecretary of state in the Reichsfinanzministerium (treasury), which confiscated the assets of murdered Jews, Fritz Reinhard—comprised approximately 450 men, predominantly noncommissioned ss officers, of whom just under 100 were delegates of Hitler's Chancellery in Berlin. They were the murder specialists from the euthanasia program whose aim had been the killing of the disabled, which had been halted in 1941. The trained specialists brought with them to Operation Reinhard their knowledge in the use of poisonous gas to commit murder.

Between the end of October and the end of December 1941 the first men arrived in Lublin. Among them was

Police Commissioner Christian Wirth, who had been active not only in the euthanasia program but also as an ingenious expert in the camp at Chelmno/Kulmhof. In December 1941 Wirth became the commandant of the first extermination camp that was set up as part of Operation Reinhard. Beginning in August 1942 he was inspector of the three concentration camps Belzec, Sobibor, and Treblinka.

The camp at Belzec in East Poland was situated close to a railway station, covered an area of 275 m by 265 m, and was divided into two sections—the arrival and administration area (camp 1) and the extermination sector (camp 2), in which barracks were set up as gas chambers. At the end of February 1942 the first transports arrived at Belzec. For several days experiments were conducted to establish how the mass killing could be conducted most effectively. Unlike at Auschwitz, Wirth, who had adequate experience in the use of exhaust fumes from his time at Chelmno/Kulmhof, decided on an autonomous extermination system in which he was not dependant on the delivery of the poisonous material from industrial companies. In Belzec Wirth also tested the system of camouflaging the installations and overwhelming and deceiving the victims. The aim was to let as little time as possible pass between the arrival of a rail transport and the final depositing of the victims in mass graves.

The German staff functioned as overseers. Ukrainian "volunteers" assisted in the extermination process, a function for which they had been instructed by the ss in Trawniki, a special training camp. The Ukrainians took on the role of guards from the arrival ramp as far as the gas chamber. They urged the victims on, beating them from the time they left the train to the site of their murder, and they supervised their undressing and the forced confiscation of property. The extermination camp at Belzec existed until the end of 1942; six hundred thousand Jews were murdered there.

From March 1942 the experience gained in Belzec was put into use in Sobibor, the second extermination camp of Operation Reinhard. It lay in a sparsely populated region and also fulfilled the most important criterium of being accessible by rail since it was connected to the main railway station in Sobibor by a sidetrack. The commandant of Sobibor was Franz Stangl, a native Austrian who had worked in the euthanasia clinic of Hartheim near Linz and, later, as the chief of Treblinka, earned the reputation of being the most assiduous camp commandant in Poland. (In 1947 he was able to escape from custody in Austria to Brasil via Syria. It was not until 1967 that he was arrested and deported to the Federal Republic, where in 1970 he was sentenced to life imprisonment for the part he played in the deaths of 900,000 Jews.)

Approximately 250,000 human beings were murdered in Sobibor in three extermination waves (May-June 1942, October-December 1942, and March 1943). One of the perpetrators, Erich Bauer, who was called the "master of gas" by the inmates for his function in the camp, reported that this result was seen as unsatisfactory by those who were immediately responsible for the killing:

In the canteen in Sobibor I once overheard a conversation between Frenzel, Stangl, and Wagner. They were talking about the number of victims in the extermination camps at Belzec, Treblinka, as well as Sobibor, and for reasons of competitiveness expressed their regret that Sobibor *an letzter Stelle rangierte* (occupied last position).

One of the murderers described his activities in the spring of 1942 in the straightforward language of the dutiful technician who carried out his assigned task with emotionless zeal. Erich Fuchs, ss noncommissioned officer, had taken a truck to collect staff from Lublin and an engine from Lemberg. The equipment for the extermination of human life was installed and made ready for operation:

When I arrived in Sobibor I saw an area near the railway station where there was a concrete building and several solid buildings. . . . We unloaded the engine. It was a heavy Russian petrol engine (presumably a tank engine or the engine from a towing vehicle) with at least 200 horsepower (a carburetor engine, six cylinder, with water cooling). We placed the engine on a concrete block and set about connecting the exhaust with the pipe. Then I tried out the engine. At first it didn't work. I repaired the ignition and the valves so that the engine finally started. The chemical engineer, whom I knew from Belzec, went into the gas chamber with a measuring instrument to test the concentration of gas. Right after that, a trial gassing was carried out. I think it's correct to say that 30–40 women were gassed in one gas chamber. The Jewesses had to get undressed in a covered outside area (in the forest) close to the gas chamber and were herded into the gas chamber by specially designated members of the ss and by Ukrainian volunteers. When the women were shut up in the gas chamber, I attended to the engine with Bauer. At first the engine idled. We both stood next to the engine and switched from "open exhaust to cell" so that the gasses were fed into the chamber. At the suggestion of the chemical engineer, I programmed the engine to a a particular number of revs per minute so that it would no longer be necessary to accelerate. After about ten minutes the 30–40 women were dead. The chemical engineer and the ss people gave me a sign to turn off the engine. I packed up my tools and watched the bodies being transported away. The transport was in the form of a rail wagon that ran from somewhere close to the gas chamber to an area far away.

With regard to the technology of extermination, Treblinka was the most perfect camp of Operation Reinhard. In terms of its size and facilities it was on a par with Sobibor. The location had been determined in spring 1942; once again decisive was the rail connection, but also important was the remoteness with possibilities of camouflage. The extermination machinery of Treblinka was in operation from July 1942 until August 1943, with the result that nine hundred thousand human lives were extinguished.

Richard Glazar, one of the few survivors of Treblinka, had been deported there via Theresienstadt. The twenty-two year old from Bohemia found a reprieve from instant death because he could be put to use as an "work Jew." For ten months, from October 1942 until August 1943, he sorted through the personal effects of the murdered, bundled their clothes, and helped to keep order in the factory of death, always prepared for his own death. He succeeded in escaping during the prisoner revolt on August 2, 1943. Accompanied by a friend, he managed to make his way across Poland and into the German Reich where, posing as a "foreign worker" in the armaments industry, he lived to see the end of the war and liberation in Mannheim. In the 1960s and 1970s Richard Glazar was one of the witnesses testifying against the perpetrators of Treblinka during their trials in the Düsseldorf district court. He was able to give an exact portrayal of the extermination camp, the "trap with the green fence," the largest murder site after Auschwitz.

This Treblinka was a small trap with a huge capacity, set up in an enclave of sand not far from the former Russian-Polish border and the River Bug. No selection, no tatoo, from the trains that rolled up they were taken straight to the "disinfection bath," to the gas chambers. The name Treblinka was borrowed from the neighboring village with its few wretched farm huts. The killing factory opened its doors in June 1942, after the first gas chambers were completed. They had a capacity of three hundred to five hundred human beings per hour. Some time in September the new gas chambers, with a far greater capacity, were put into operation. In a brick building five "shower rooms" in each chamber were arranged along a central corridor. Into each room you could push one hundred people in forty minutes, so that in all ten rooms one thousand people could be gassed at any one time. For the gassing, cyclon B was not used as it was in Auschwitz, but simply exhaust fumes from the engines of stolen Russian tanks.

In an area of approximately only 400 m by 600 m, up to fifteen thousand human beings disappeared daily—just ceased to exist. . . . The two sections of Treblinka were kept strictly separated. A high wall of sand ran between the two. In the first, larger section there was the entrance ramp, the disrobing square, the sorting area with the enormous piles of all manner of things from the transports and the barracks for this section. Adjacent to this so-called reception camp were the night barracks of the Arbeitsjuden, the barracks where the ss lived, and the command headquarters. The smaller, second section was the actual death camp. You were not allowed to call it that, however. The ss people only ever spoke of "camp 2." That's where the gas chambers, the pits for the corpses, the large grill for burning bodies made from railway tracks, and more night barracks for the Arbeitsjuden were. . . . After a few days I already knew exactly what happened to our transport and what in fact happened to all transports that arrived in Treblinka. Even before reaching the entrance gate a certain number of carriages are uncoupled on the single-tracked railway siding. Sometimes five hundred, but sometimes a thousand people inside. The locomotive pushes the carriages slowly in through the gate. What happens after that as people are getting off is what I experienced myself: "Everyone out, quicker—take hand luggage with you, leave heavy bags behind, it will be sent on after you!" The mass of people is led via the entrance ramp to the disrobing area. It's the green, fenced in square, where we had to take all our clothes off for the disinfection bath. "Men to the right, women with children to the left!" I was still standing there with them, already undressed, before I was taken out and led away. The women were led into the "hairdressers," where their hair was shaven off. They are supposed to have made gaskets for engines from the women's hair. In the meantime the men, already naked, had to pile up the hand luggage that they had brought with them in the corner of the disrobing square that was closest to the sorting area. The ss made sure they worked in double time. The lungs then breathe more deeply and you get to the gas chamber more quickly. Everyone—the shorn women with children and the panting men—were then herded together through the "tube" into the second section of the camp. The tube was a narrow passageway of barbed wire, which reminded me of the sluice that wild animals have to go through into an arena. Only this passageway was longer, went around a bend, and you could not see in or out. The barbed wire was thick and intertwined with green twigs, as, by the way, was the rest of the fencing around Treblinka. At the border between the two sections of the camp the "little cashier's office" was built directly into the passageway. At the counter of this small wooden booth everyone had to hand over their documents, watches, and jewelry. At this point your name was taken, a little further on your naked, nameless life.

The large majority of Polish Jews fell victim to Operation Reinhardt in the three camps at Belzec, Sobibor, and Treblinka. But Jews from Western Europe—from Holland and France—as well as from Austria and Slovakia were also murdered in Sobibor.

In July 1942 Himmler ordered the final day of the operation to be December 31, 1942. Notwithstanding their pronounced sense of duty, the killing commandos could not manage that. It was only at the beginning of November 1943 that Globocnik reported to Himmler: "On the 19.10.43 I concluded Operation Reinhardt, which I had waged in the General Government, and dissolved all the camps."

The last months had been devoted to erasing all traces of the murders. The specialists from Sonderkommando 1005 under ss-Standartenführer Blobel had already had firsthand experience with the exhumation of bodies from mass graves. The corpses were lifted out of the pits with bulldozers and then burned on grating made out of railway tracks. Whatever was left over was ground down in bone mills. Ashes and bone remains were finally tossed back into the pits.

Belzec was the first camp to be closed down. On order from Himmler, Sobibor was converted into a concentration camp in which stolen ammunition was stored and sorted. In Treblinka a last work detachment of "work Jews" tore down barracks and fences before they were all shot. The ground was ploughed up, trees were planted. Ukrainians from the camp staff set up home in the newly established farmsteads.

In the course of the year 1942 the extermination capacity of Auschwitz had been increased to such an extent that the camps of Operation Reinhard were no longer needed. Auschwitz was now set up to receive the transports from all countries under National Socialist rule and to murder, in a completely rationalized procedure, the Jews who arrived in the deportation trains. In spring 1944 the Hungarian Jews were the last large group to experience the fate of the Final Solution.

The goal of annihilating all the Jews of Europe, as it was proclaimed at the conference in the villa Am Grossen Wannsee in January 1942, was not reached. Yet the six million murder victims make the Holocaust a unique crime in the history of mankind. This number of victims—and with certainty the following represent the minimum number in each case—cannot express that adequately. Numbers are just too abstract. However they must be stated in order to make clear the dimension of the genocide: 165,000 Jews from Germany, 65,000 from Austria, 32,000 from France and Belgium, more than 100,000 from the Netherlands, 60,000 from Greece, the same number from Yugoslavia, more than 140,000 from Czechoslovakia, half a million from Hungary, 2.2 million from the Soviet Union, and 2.7 million from Poland. To these numbers must be added all those killed in the pogroms and massacres in Romania and Transistrien (over 200,000) and the deported and murdered Jews from Albania and Norway, Denmark and Italy, from Luxembourg and Bulgaria. Directly or indirectly they all lost their lives as the result of National Socialist racial ideology, which was proclaimed and submissively pursued by the German master race.

Even half a century after the crime the question must be asked as to how much the Germans knew of the Holocaust.

Himmler spoke repeatedly, and without the use of the usual covert language, about the murder of the Jews as a fait accompli. In October 1943 he explained to high-ranking functionaries in the NSDAP in Posen the ideologically justified obligation to commit genocide:

The sentence The Jews must be eradicated, with its few words, gentlemen, is easily uttered. For the one who has to perform the duties that it demands, it is the most onerous and most difficult thing there is. . . . We are confronted with the question: What about the women and children? I have decided to find a very clear solution to that as well. You see, I didn't consider I had the right to eradicate the men—that is, to kill them or have them killed—and leave the children to grow up and take revenge on our sons and grandsons. The difficult decision had to be made that this people should disappear from the face of the earth.

He also spoke about the Jewish Question to generals from the army and, to intense applause from the officers, proclaimed: "It was solved in an uncompromising manner befitting the fight for survival of our people, a fight for the existence of our blood. I speak to you about it as a friend."

Of course it cannot be concluded from Himmler's open grumblings about the murder of the Jews in front of officers and functionaries of the Nazi regime that the majority of Germans knew about the Holocaust. But there were many opportunities to hear about it and it was, in fact, difficult to avoid knowing. Soldiers in the army told about the eastern front while at home on holiday or wrote home about what they had seen. It was just as difficult to conceal the existence of the ghettos and concentration camps as it was the deportation of the Jews from all corners of Europe "for settlement in the East."

That there was definite knowledge that went beyond rumors about the organized genocide on the eastern border of the German sphere of power is evident. But the Germans knew about the gas chambers and extermination camps without wanting to know about them. What for many was self-protection turned into the greatest sham of a generation after the collapse of the Hitler state. Because they were horrified and ashamed of the crimes, they did not wish to have shared the responsibility by knowing about them. After 1945 they protested with one voice that they had known nothing and convinced themselves that the genocide had been the terrible secret of a small band of criminals.

For half a century legal experts and historians have occupied themselves with the Holocaust. Some with the unpromising but, at the same time, very necessary attempt to see justice served on earth, to have the perpetrators punished. Others with the difficult search for details of the truth. The many court proceedings, from the Nuremberg trials to the Eichmann trial in Jerusalem in 1961, the Auschwitz trial in the mid-1960s, and the Treblinka trials in Düssldorf, have served to show the limitations of the law. However, they have contributed enormously to an understanding of the events, to a greater knowledge of the Holocaust.

Despite the plethora of studies and documentation, which initially served the securing of evidence and then the portrayal of the events that had taken place, historians are still faced with the task of explaining the causes and purpose of the crime. Was the Holocaust the logical and therefore a priori consequence of the ideology of anti-semitism and the superiority of the Teutonic world, was it part of a cool and calculated politics of power that presup-posed movements of populations and planned as part of its strategy the annihilation of certain populations, was it Hitler's intention from the very beginning, or was the murder of the Jews a consequence of the radicalization of National Socialist rule or simply the result of opportunities that arose? There can be no doubts about the facts of the Holocaust; the search for an explanation in keeping with human moral values and reason continues.

BIBLIOGRAPHY

Browning, Christopher R. *Ordinary Men: Reserve Police Battalion 101 and the Final Solution.* New York: Harper-Collins, 1992.

The reconstruction of the operations of a police unit in 1942–1943 and, at the same time, an excellent case study of the psychology of the perpetrators.

Burrin, Philippe. *Hitler and the Jews: The Genesis of the Holocaust.* London: Edward Arnold, 1994.

The portrayal of Hitler's ideology and motives in the decision to exterminate the Jews in fall 1941.

Czech, Danuta. *Auschwitz Chronicle, 1939–1945.* New York: Henry Holt, 1990.

A chronology of the extermination camp compiled from records and other sources.

Encyclopedia of the Holocaust. Israel Gutman, editor in chief. New York: Macmillan, 1990.

Unfortunately, numerous errors and mistakes limit the usefulness considerably.

Glazar, Richard. *Trap with a Green Fence: Survival in Treblinka.* Evanston, Ill.: Northwestern University Press, 1995.

An autobiographical report by one of the few survivors of the extermination camp; the methods of the Holocaust; the prisoners' revolt in August 1943.

Hilberg, Raul. *The Destruction of the European Jews.* Chicago: Quadrangle, 1961.
The most important and factual work on the topic.

Hilberg, Raul, Stanislaw Staron, and Josef Kermisz, eds. *The Warsaw Diary of Adam Czerniakow: Prelude to Doom.* New York: Stein and Day, 1979.
Notebooks of the chairman of the Warsaw Judenrat on the daily life under Gestapo terror in the ghetto.

Hoess, Rudolf. *Commandant of Auschwitz: The Autobiography of Rudolf Hoess.* Cleveland: World, 1959.
Depiction of the life and career of the concentration camp commandant with detailed descriptions of the extermination process, written in 1946–1947 in the Kraków prison at the time of the court trial.

Klee, Ernst, Willi Dressen, Volker Riess, eds. *"The Good Old Days": The Holocaust as Seen by Its Perpetrators and Bystanders.* New York: Free, 1991.
A documentary history of the Holocaust from the perspective of the perpetrator, compiled from documents of the Central Office of the State Justice Administration.

Kogon, Eugon, Hermann Langbein, and Adalbert Rückerl, eds. *Nazi Mass Murder: A Documentary History of the Use of Poison Gas.* New Haven: Yale University Press, 1993.

A detailed study by an international team of experts on all the problems of murder by gas during the Holocaust.

Krausnick, Helmut, Hans Buchheim, Martin Broszat, and Hans-Adolf Jacobsen. *Anatomy of the SS State.* New York: Walker, 1968.

Expert opinion submitted by the Institute for Contemporary History (Munich) for the Auschwitz Trial; a well-documented account of the persecution of the Jews (Krausnick), the SS as an instrument of power (Buchheim), and the mass executions of Soviet prisoners of war (Jacobsen) are still valid.

Langbein, Hermann. *Against All Hope: Resistance in the Nazi Concentration Camps, 1938–1945.* New York: Paragon House, 1993.

Meticulously researched and documented portrayal of resistance in concentration and extermination camps.

Levi, Primo. *Is This a Man?* New York: Orion, 1959.

A literary account of life as a work prisoner in Auschwitz, first published in 1958 in Italian.

Marszalek, Josef. *Majdanek, the Concentration Camp in Lublin.* Warsaw: Interpress, 1986.

Heavily factual and well-documented portrayal of the Lublin-Majdanek Camp.

Nyiszli, Miklos. *Auschwitz: A Doctor's Eyewitness Account.* New York: Fawcett, 1960.

An autobiographical account written in 1946 by a member of the prisoner Sonderkommando of the crematoria in Auschwitz.

Additional titles

Breitman, Richard. *The Architect of Genocide: Himmler and the Final Solution.* New York: Knopf, 1991.

The authoritative study on the central role of Himmler in the final solution.

Friedlander, Saul. *Nazi Germany and the Jews.* Vol. 1. *The Years of Persecution, 1933–1939.* New York: HarperCollins, 1997.

Focusing on the intertwining of policy and ideology, the book offers a new perspective on the emergence of the final solution.

Lifton, Robert Jay. *The Nazi Doctors: Medical Killing and the Psychology of the Genocide.* New York: Basic, 1986.

An attempt at psychological analysis and explanation of physicians who became perpetrators during the Third Reich.

Lodz Ghetto: Inside a Community Under Siege. Compiled and edited by Alan Adelson and Robert Lapides. New York: Viking, 1989.

A compelling collection of personal writings, photographs, and documents on Jewish life and suffering in the ghetto.

Tec, Nechama. *When Light Pierced the Darkness: Christian Rescue of Jews in Nazi-Occupied Poland.* New York: Oxford University Press, 1986.

A study of rescuers' actions and motivations in helping Jews survive in German-occupied Poland.

Trunk, Isaiah. *Judenrat: The Jewish Councils in Eastern Europe Under Nazi Occupation.* New York: Stein and Day, 1972.

A thoroughly documented study of Jewish councils, their inter-nal organization, and their attempt to alleviate the plight of Jews in the face of German persecution.

Yahil, Leni. *The Holocaust: The Fate of European Jewry, 1932–1945.* New York: Oxford University Press, 1990.
A comprehensive description of German extermination policies and Jewish responses.

Wyman, David. *The Abandonment of the Jews: America and the Holocaust 1941–1945.* New York: Pantheon, 1984.
A study of America's role in the Holocaust, raising controversial issues and depicting an American government deeply rooted in antisemitism.

Journals

Holocaust and Genocide Studies. Oxford University Press, in association with the United States Holocaust Memorial Museum.

INDEX

Adler, H. G., 112
Adler-Rudel, Salomon, 19–20
Agudas Jisroel, 19
Alaska, as Jewish reserve, 68
Albania, number of Jews killed
　from, 153
Alexanderplatz, 115
Aliyah Bet, 37
Alter, Leon, 66
American Joint Distribution
　Committee, 20
Am Grossen Wannsee, Wannsee
　Conference at, 1
Annihilation, see Final Solution
　(Endlösung)
Antisemitenspiegel, 68
Antisemitism: alliances among
　Jewish organizations and,
　19–22; basis for, 14–16; Ein-
　satzgruppen taking advantage
　of, 76; emigration of Jews
　and spread of, 35; in foreign
　Jewish press, 16–17; German
　invasion of Poland and, 43;
　German Jewish response to,
　16–18; German press and,

30–31; international Jewish
　conspiracy and, 61; as official
　state doctrine, 16; in Poland,
　43, 45, 48, 50; Reichskristall-
　nacht and, 29
Ariergesetzgebung (Aryan legis-
　lation), 109
Armaments industry: forced
　labor in, 14, 40; in Lodz
　ghetto, 52, 57; in Warsaw
　ghetto, 49
Army: as absent from Wannsee
　Conference, 3; Eastern Euro-
　pean Jews shot by, 3, 8; Jews
　excluded from, 25; Serbian
　Jews and gypsies shot by
　(October 1941), 8, 86–87;
　see also World War I;
　World War II
Aryan clause, 25
Aryanization, of German econ-
　omy, 32–33, 39–40
Assets, see Expropriation
Association for Jewish Culture,
　see Jüdischer Kulturbund
Aumühle, 95, 97

Transit camps, 12; deportation of
Jews to, 92, 93; Gypsies in,
127; *see also* Theresienstadt
Trawiniki transit camp, deportation of Jews to, 93
Trawniki training camp, 145
Treblinka extermination camp,
13, 144, 147–51; Bialystok
inmates murdered in, 60; con-
version of to farm, 152;
deportation of Jews from
Theresienstadt to, 118; gas
chambers in, 149, 150; Gypsies murdered in, 129; number
of Jews murdered at, 148;
procedure used in, 147,
148–51; Stangl as comman-
dant of, 145; transport of
Jews to, 93
Trials, 155; Auschwitz (1964),
129, 155; of Paul Blobel, 84;
in Cracow, 133; of Adolf
Eichmann (1961), 155; of
Rudolf Hess, 133; Nurem-
berg (1948), 84, 133, 139; of
Karl Rahm, 119; of Dr.
Siegfried Seidl, 119; of Sonderkommando 42 murderer,
81–82; of Franz Stangl, 145;
of Theresienstadt comman-
dants, 119; Treblinka, 155
Tschenstochau, ghettos of, 58

Uebehelhoer, Friedrich, 50, 51
Ukraine: Auxiliary Police from,

76; Einsatzgruppen murdering Jews in, 64, 75, 78–84;
Einsatzkommando murdering
Jews in, 59; ghettos of, 58;
Gypsies murdered in, 129–30;
loss of citizenship and expropriation for Jews in, 90
Ukrainians: assisting in Belzec
extermination camp, 144–45;
assisting in Treblinka extermination camp, 152; Gypsies
murdered by, 130; Jews murdered by, 77–84
United States: Central Committee aided by, 20; emigration
to, 20, 35, 37–38
Universities, ban on Jewish doctorate students in, 26
Upper Silesia, deportation of
Jews to Auschwitz from, 136
Ustashifascists, Gypsies murdered
by, 130

Vehicles, Jews prohibited from
owning/driving, 41
Verordnung zur Ausschaltung
der Juden aus dem deutschen
Wirtschaftsleben (decree
expelling Jews from German
financial sector), 39
Versailles, Treaty of, Madagascar
project and, 72
Vichy government, Jews from
Baden and Saarland Palatinate
interned by, 91